CHRISTIANS AND
THEIR MANY IDENTITIES
IN LATE ANTIQUITY,
NORTH AFRICA,
200–450 CE

CHRISTIANS AND THEIR MANY IDENTITIES IN LATE ANTIQUITY, NORTH AFRICA, 200–450 CE

ÉRIC REBILLARD

CORNELL UNIVERSITY PRESS
Ithaca and London

Copyright © 2012 by Cornell University

All rights reserved. Except for brief quotations in a review, this book, or parts thereof, must not be reproduced in any form without permission in writing from the publisher. For information, address Cornell University Press, Sage House, 512 East State Street, Ithaca, New York 14850.

First published 2012 by Cornell University Press
First printing, Cornell Paperbacks, 2017

Library of Congress Cataloging-in-Publication Data

Rebillard, Éric.
  Christians and their many identities in late antiquity, North Africa, 200–450 CE / Éric Rebillard.
     p. cm.
  Includes bibliographical references and index.
  ISBN 978-0-8014-5142-3 (cloth : alk. paper)
  ISBN 978-1-5017-1357-6 (pbk. : alk. paper)
  1. Africa, North—Church history. 2. Church history—Primitive and early church, ca. 30–600. 3. Christian life—History—Early church, ca. 30–600. I. Title.
  BR190.R43 2013
  276.1′02—dc23   2012020509

Cornell University Press strives to use environmentally responsible suppliers and materials to the fullest extent possible in the publishing of its books. Such materials include vegetable-based, low-VOC inks and acid-free papers that are recycled, totally chlorine-free, or partly composed of nonwood fibers. For further information, visit our website at www.cornellpress.cornell.edu.

Contents

Acknowledgments vii
Note on Primary Sources ix

Introduction	1
1. Setting the Stage: Carthage at the End of the Second Century	9
2. Persecution and the Limits of Religious Allegiance	34
3. Being Christian in the Age of Augustine	61
Conclusion	92

Notes 99
Bibliography 109
Index 127

Acknowledgments

The research for this book started (too long ago) in the very congenial and productive context of the program Les identités religieuses dans les mondes grec et romain d'Alexandre à Justinien, directed by Nicole Belayche and Simon Mimouni (Paris, 2001–2005). Mark Vessey's invitation to contribute a chapter to his *Companion to Augustine* came at the right time to set me back to work on the topic of being Christian in late antiquity. The conceptual framework of the project was refined and tuned during a graduate seminar at Cornell University in 2010. With their patience and inquisitiveness the participants helped me tighten up my approach. Jörg Rüpke's generous invitation to join the Max-Weber Kolleg für kultur- und sozialwissenschaftliche Studien (Erfurt Universität) as a fellow in 2010–2011 provided invaluable time for writing and audiences for discussion. I thank all the fellows, students, and staff members of the MWK for welcoming me and my family in Erfurt and making our year there so fruitful. I also thank Jörg for reading the first draft of the whole book and making many insightful comments. The final version of the book was written—and many references checked—in Oxford. I thank Neil McLynn for facilitating my election as Visiting Scholar at Corpus Christi for Michaelmas and Hilary Terms. Special thanks are due to the chair of the department of classics, Charles Brittain, to the dean of the College of Arts and Science, and to the provost of Cornell University for allowing and funding a second year of leave. I owe encouragements and forceful comments to Claire Sotinel who read a very early draft of the introduction and first two chapters. Peter Brown was inspirational early in the project, when he directed my attention to Rogers Brubaker's ethnographical work. I wish I could have included all the conclusions he invited me to draw after reading the final draft of the book. I must acknowledge the invaluable work of Alice Brigance, who not only carefully edited my English text but also helped me clarify many points with her questions and comments. Linda Brown's help has been vital, fetching books or articles left in my office at Cornell and sending scanned versions of them almost instantaneously. Last, but not least, my thanks go to my wife, Suzanne, and my son, Emile, who cheerfully followed me to Germany and England!

❧ Note on Primary Sources

Abbreviations for works are those of the *Thesaurus Linguae Latinae* for Latin texts and of the *Diccionario Griego-Español (DGE)* for Greek texts. Translations are mine unless otherwise acknowledged in the notes.

Introduction

Binary oppositions between Christians and non-Christians are now increasingly understood as a discursive construct, part of the making of a Christian identity (see, among others, Lieu 2004, Kahlos 2007, and Perkins 2009), and therefore it has become apparent that on-the-ground confessional identities are less important than contemporary sources state. However, our view of the realities beyond the discursive structures has not yet been thoroughly reexamined. Scholars acknowledge the difference between the social experience and the discursive construct of our sources, but their focus is mainly on discourse. This state of affairs is partly the result of the relatively recent conversion of the field to the so-called linguistic or cultural turn:[1] early Christian studies are now experiencing the disaffection for social history that historical studies of other periods have known and overcome (see Spiegel 2005; Sewell 2005). The field is at the stage when most scholars either deliberately do not use texts as evidence of an "extra-textual social reality" or, if they do, they ignore that this is not a straightforward process. I would like to explore alternative interpretive approaches.

Beyond "Groupism"

The study of early Christianity made significant progress when the interactions of religious groups, rather than their activities in isolation, became the preferred object of investigation. The volume edited by Judith Lieu, John

North, and Tessa Rajak in 1992, *The Jews among Pagans and Christians: In the Roman Empire*, was seminal in this respect, and there is now a long list of books and papers that associate these three religious groups in their titles.[2] However, this approach also tends to reify these groups—despite postmodern and generally pro forma observations that their boundaries are contingent and fluctuating—and we continue, consequently, to treat religious conflicts as encounters between religious groups. The risk here is that we uncritically adopt categories of religious practice as our categories of social analysis, as Rogers Brubaker warns in his discussion of ethnic conflicts and categories of ethnopolitical practice (2002: 166). This is what he defines as "groupism": "the tendency to take discrete, sharply differentiated, internally homogeneous and externally bounded groups as basic constituents of social life, chief protagonists of social conflicts, and fundamental units of social analysis" (164). This tendency is all the more prevalent in the study of early Christians, since our evidence, largely texts written by clerics, constructs Christian identity as that of an internally homogeneous and externally bounded group (see Perkins 2009 on this construction).

In order to avoid starting our analysis with the assumption of groups, Brubaker suggests that we focus instead on "the processes through which categories are used by individuals to make sense of the social world" (2002: 170). He then proposes that we consider "groupness" rather than groups and treat "groupness" as a type of contingent *event* (168), arguing that, even when "groupness" does occur, it lasts "only for a passing moment" (182). Such are the principles that define "everyday ethnicity" in his study of the workings of ethnicity and nationhood in the Transylvanian Romanian town of Cluj between 1995 and 2001 (Brubaker et al. 2006; see Fox and Miller-Idris 2008). Brubaker and his students embrace Eric Hobsbawm's dictum that phenomena such as ethnicity and nationhood "cannot be understood unless also analyzed from below" (Hobsbawm 1990: 10). The goal is not so much to oppose "elite" discourses to "popular" practices as it is to balance the impression of the centrality of ethnicity presented by political discourse with the experiential centrality (or not) of ethnicity in everyday life. Brubaker and his students are interested in what they call "the intermittency of ethnicity," seeking how and when ethnicity is relevant, looking for "sites where ethnicity might—but need not—be at work" (Brubaker et al. 2006: 168). As they warn, "in order to understand *how* ethnicity matters ... it is important to bear in mind *how little* it matters to much of everyday experience" (206). However, they are very careful to point out that the fundamental intermittency and the episodic character of ethnicity must not be analyzed as a measure of its importance or even of its significance (362–363). What matters to them in the end is "the disjuncture between the thematization of ethnicity and nationhood in the political realm and their experience and enactment in everyday life" (363).

The disjuncture between the thematization of ethnicity and its enactment in everyday life is of immediate relevance to my project. Because of the nature of our sources, for the most part texts written by the clergy, scholars have tended to frame their questions in terms of Christian interactions, and, unsurprisingly, they have arrived at conclusions delimited by Christian considerations. To give but one example: any attempt to study "Christian burial" can only, and in a way preemptively (see Fox and Miller-Idris 2008 about "nationally framed questions"), lead to a focus on exclusively Christian places of burial. However, as I have shown, many Christians did not consider their Christianity relevant to their choice of a burial place (Rebillard 2009b). The findings of Brubaker and his students regarding ethnicity and nationhood also suggest that we should no longer assume that the behavior of Christians was predominantly determined by their religious allegiance (despite the demands of the bishops). They also indicate that we should instead ask how and in which contexts Christianness became salient in Christians' everyday life.[3]

The "Internal Plurality" of the Individual

The decision to abandon groups as the basic units of social analysis is consistent with recent attempts by sociologists to promote a sociology at the level of the individual.[4] Thus Bernard Lahire suggests discarding the "homogenizing perspective on individuals in society" dominant in the social sciences (he mentions sociology, historiography, and anthropology) for "a more complex vision of the individual as being less unified and as the bearer of heterogeneous habits, schemes, or dispositions which may be contrary or even contradictory to one another" (2003: 344). This leads him to introduce the notion of an individual's "internal plurality" (see Lahire 2011). He also calls for consideration of multiple contexts of action, setting himself apart from the majority of sociologists, who study how individuals act within one specific arena. Thus the program of a sociology at the level of the individual is to "identify the internal plurality of individuals and the way it acts and 'distributes' itself according to various social contexts" (Lahire 2003: 346). Lahire concludes with a new understanding of social agents: "Social agents are not made all of one piece; *they are fit together from separate parts, complex charts of dispositions to act and to believe which are more or less tightly constituted*. This does not mean that they 'lack coherence', but that they lack a principle of unique coherence—of *beliefs, i.e., models, norms, ideals, values, and of dispositions of act*" (348). This contrasts quite sharply with the claims of the bishops of late antiquity that Christians act according to the unique principle of coherence that the bishops themselves provide in explaining Christianity.

It has been a common idea that individuals have multiple identities since at least William James (James 1890 on the "selves"), but the relationships between and among identities have seldom been theorized (see Burke 2003: 195). Identity theory is one approach that can provide us with some basic terms and definitions (even if its emphasis on quantitative analysis ultimately makes it of little use to ancient historians).[5] Identity theory defines identities as "meanings" that individuals hold for themselves based on category memberships (social identities), on roles (role identities), or on their "biological entities" (personal identities). The "salience" of an identity is its probability of being activated in a situation, and "activation" refers to the condition in which an identity is actively engaged, as opposed to being latent and inactive. Identity theory also provides useful insights into the conditions under which multiple identities are activated, and thus refines the model in which only one identity is activated at any one moment. Peter Burke (2003) argues that an individual may hold multiple identities within a single group and within intersecting groups. Within a single group, a person can have several identities: for example, a man can identify both as a father and as a son in an extended family group. Another case is "when a person has an activated identity in a group and something in the situation activates an identity that the person has in another group" (201). Multiple identities in intersecting groups occur when different groups, in which an individual has different identities, overlap (202). Such distinctions will be useful when we attempt to understand potential conflicts of identities within individuals in late antiquity.

Because of the nature of our evidence (see below), we will focus our analysis on identities based on category memberships such as ethnicity, religion, and occupation. Each category membership exists as a family or "set" of contrastive categories in a given culture (Handelman 1977: 191). In the religious set, during the period here under consideration, we find, among others, Christian, Jewish, and pagan. Two types of arrangement of category membership sets, lateral and hierarchical, can be distinguished: "Given a lateral arrangement, the assumption is that various category sets (i.e. ethnic, occupational, religious, educational, etc.) are interchangeable to a certain extent in an occasion of interaction; and therefore, that the same person can be categorized according to different criteria of relevance in different situations. But if the arrangement of membership sets tends more to the hierarchical, then all categorizations about a person may be allocated according to, and interpreted in terms of, membership in a given category set" (Handelman 1977: 192–193). In a hierarchical arrangement, if religious membership is given salience, the entirety of an individual's behavior should be determined and interpreted in terms of his or her religious affiliation. In a lateral arrangement, situational selection is key, and different category membership sets can be activated according to the context of the interaction. This distinction between types of arrangement will be particularly useful when we compare the point of view of Christians to that of their bishops.

The Evidence and Its Limits

Before I describe how the theoretical considerations outlined above inform my study of North African Christians between the end of the second century and the middle of the fifth century, some issues related to the nature of the evidence need to be discussed.

I will start by distinguishing having direct evidence on individuals as opposed to taking individuals into account in our analysis. It is a fact that we have very little direct evidence on individuals,[6] and I should add that, when we do have it, as in the case of Augustine, for instance, it is extremely difficult to use (see BeDuhn 2010). However, the lack of direct evidence does not justify ignoring individuals and taking groups to be the sole unit of analysis. In fact, evidence on group life can be read with individuals as the focal point. Instead of assuming the grouping and its constancy, I will try to ascertain when and how individuals do form groups, when attempts to form a group fail, and so on. This suffices to suggest that we do not need direct evidence on individuals in order to take them into account.

A further difficulty with our evidence is that it consists mainly of texts written by members of the clergy. In light of this limitation, I will first address the textual or discursive nature of our evidence. A positive consequence of the linguistic or cultural turn is that we are now more aware of the delicate correlation between discursive constructs and social experience. This has made it impossible to defend what Dominick LaCapra called the "documentary model" (1985: 18–20) with its referential notion of evidence in which facts speak for themselves. However, we can agree that texts should not be read as uncomplicated representations of an external reality, without also renouncing the use of texts to approach an extratextual social reality. As Gabrielle Spiegel has pointed out, extratextual pressures are at work within texts, along with inter- and intratextual forces (1990: 84; see Clark 1998: 12–13). Hence the attention to what she called the "social logic" of texts.

Some texts are more the products of extratextual pressures than others. By saying this, I do not mean to revert to the opposition between "documents" and other texts. In the case of sermons or pastoral treatises, for example, there is no doubt that these texts construct an audience that has no exact reflection in social reality. At the same time, in order for the process of communication to happen, interaction must take place, and, as the pragmatics of communication suggests, the "transmitter" should not receive exclusive attention, but processes such as feedback must also be considered (Watzlawick, Beavin, and Jackson 1967). It is my contention that sermons and pastoral treatises participate in processes of communication that leave direct and indirect traces in the texts themselves, and that the practice of "symptomatic reading" or reading "against the grain" allows us to recover these traces.

From this perspective, the fact that most of our sources are written by members of the clergy ceases to be such an important limitation. Not only are we able to analyze the ways in which the clergy construct an audience, and through this deconstruction catch a glimpse of some extratextual reality, but we are also able to discern within their texts the marks of the communicative processes in which they are engaged, and therefore of the individuals with whom they interact.

North Africa, 150–450 CE

Rescaling to the level of the individual goes hand in hand with the localized focus that has been advocated for some time now in the study of Christianity (Christian 1981; Frankfurter 2005 offers a forceful plea for the late antique period). Why North Africa? The answer lies in the relative abundance of sources for a relatively continuous period of time. There is no epigraphic or archaeological record of Christians before the fourth century (Barnes 1985: 280–282), but the works of Tertullian at the end of the second century and of Cyprian in the middle of the third provide ample evidence. These two authors supply the bulk of the material for chapters 1 and 2. With the exception of the sources on the "Great Persecution" analyzed in chapter 2, I do not deal with the fourth century, because of the lack of evidence. Among the writers of North African origin listed in volume 3 of Paul Monceaux's monumental *Histoire littéraire de l'Afrique chrétienne*, which covers fourth-century evidence not related to the Donatist schism, only Arnobius lived in North Africa. However, he did not survive for long after the end of the "Great Persecution."[7] All the other texts preserved for the fourth century are connected to the Donatist schism. These allow us to reconstruct the ecclesiology of the Donatists and their opponents, but generally only the clergy appear in these texts, and we cannot get a sense of how laypeople conceived of their own identities. This becomes possible again only with the letters and sermons of Augustine, that is, for the period between 395 and 430. This is the material I analyze in chapter 3, along with some epigraphic and archaeological evidence.[8]

In chapter 1 ("Setting the Stage: Carthage at the End of the Second Century"), I focus on Tertullian and the evidence on Carthage at the turn of the third century. It is commonly noted that Tertullian's depiction of Christians differs according to whether a given text is targeted to a pagan audience or to Christians. For example, in the *Apology* Christians are presented as unexceptional and present in all social groups throughout the city, distinct only in their exclusive religious allegiance to the Christian God, whereas in *On Idolatry* every manner of social interaction is described as a possible source of pollution for Christians. Not only must such a reading of *On Idolatry* be strongly nuanced (see Stroumsa 1998 and below), but Tertullian's prescriptions themselves reveal that Christians did not belong to a "separate world." Attention to Tertullian's very selective focus on Christianness and to the dialogic nature of his treatises allows me to show that Christianness mattered only intermittently in Christians' everyday life. Not only did Christians share a number of identities with non-Christians, but Christians and non-Christians alike did not necessarily or consistently regard their religious allegiance as more significant than other identities.

Chapter 2 ("Persecution and the Limits of Religious Allegiance") is an attempt to evaluate the degree of groupness associated with the category "Christians." I move from an analysis of when and how Christianness mattered at the level of the individual to an analysis of when and how Christianness was a basis for group-formation. I consider, in particular, how Christians responded when they were targeted as a group by outsiders. This chapter accordingly reviews episodes of persecution in North Africa from the end of the second until the beginning of the fourth century. The picture that emerges is consistent with the conclusions reached in chapter 1: it appears that, in spite of their leaders' incitement to do so, Christians seldom opposed a communal response to the persecutors, and that a significant number of them chose to suspend, if only temporarily, their Christian membership. Additionally, when Decius gave the order that all inhabitants of the Roman Empire must sacrifice to the gods for restoration of order and security, the majority of Christians complied. They considered the sacrifice a requirement of their membership in the imperial commonwealth, and they did not activate their Christian membership in this context. On the other hand, with the emergence of the strong figure of a "monarchical bishop," we see

Christians bonding around their leader, a tendency that is strengthened in the following period.

Chapter 3 ("Being Christian in the Age of Augustine") proceeds with an analysis of everyday Christianity in the Theodosian period, and the core of the material I consider are letters and sermons of Augustine. The richness of the evidence, especially the arguments Christians used when their bishop challenged them to justify their behavior, grants us abundant insights into Christians' self-understanding. I also show that tensions between bishop and Christians regarding the limits of religious allegiance were not due to competing hierarchies of commitments, but to the fact that most Christians practiced a situational selection of identities; that is, they did not give salience to their Christianness at all times. The mechanisms of selection can be described rather precisely through the study of a few letter exchanges preserved in the correspondence of Augustine. Toward the end of the chapter, in an attempt to understand whether and how groupness occurred, I review episodes that have usually been constructed as religious conflicts between clearly defined "pagans" and "Christians." Augustine did use these categories to cast situations in terms of religious conflict, and successfully mobilized Christians in support of his agendas. However, he also unambiguously betrays his knowledge that such mobilization was only intermittent and that most Christians deactivated their Christianness once outside the church.

In the conclusion, I offer some broader observations and assess the benefits of my approach beyond North Africa.

 CHAPTER 1

Setting the Stage
Carthage at the End of the Second Century

In his magisterial study of Tertullian, Timothy Barnes notes: "It can surely be no accident that Tertullian's three earliest extant works are *De Spectaculis*, *De Idololatria* and what appears in modern editions as the second book of *De Cultu Feminarum*. All three address themselves to similar problems: how ought Christians to live out a life of faith in a pagan society?" (1985: 93). To present the conciliation of Christian faith and social life in Carthage at the end of the second century as a problem is to implicitly adopt Tertullian's own point of view. Indeed, most scholars have underestimated how crucial it was to Tertullian's rhetorical strategy to challenge Christians on this "problem." In this chapter, I will show that not all Christians saw conciliation as an issue, as Christianness was only one of the multiple identities that mattered in their everyday life.

Tertullian and the Christian Organization(s) in Carthage

Little is known about Tertullian himself. Our main sources of information are a notice of Jerome in the *De viris illustribus* (53) and various remarks in Tertullian's own works.[1] The dates of his birth and death are uncertain, but we do know that he wrote during the reigns of Septimius Severus (193–211) and Caracalla (211–217). Tertullian was born in Carthage, where he also spent most of his life. He was not raised as a Christian, but we have no details of his conversion. His writings attest to a good education, and he was very likely of equestrian status (Schöllgen 1985: 183–184). Current scholarship rejects the identification with the jurist Tertullianus.

Jerome says that Tertullian was a presbyter of the church of Carthage, and this statement was for a long time viewed in the light of his later alleged schism with the Montanists, or the New Prophecy, a movement originating in Phrygia (Trevett 1996). Nowadays, scholars tend to reject the claim that Tertullian was a schismatic as anachronistic (Mattei 1990; see Rankin 1995). His sympathy for the prophetic movement and growing dissatisfaction with the Christians he calls the *psychici* do not imply an official separation, especially in an ecclesiastical context where the relations between Christian organizations were rather fluid (Mattei 1990; Van der Lof 1991; Brent 1995). Although Tertullian was familiar with the ecclesiastical hierarchy of bishop, presbyters, and deacons (see, for instance, *bapt.* 17; see also Mattei 2000), this does not make it the case that there was one bishop overseeing all the Christians of Carthage. Indeed, we know very little about Carthaginian bishops before Cyprian: one Optatus is mentioned in the *Passio Perpetuae* 13.1, and one Agrippinus is referred to by Cyprian in context of a synod held probably around 230 (Clarke 1989: 196–199; Y. Duval 2005: 59, 107–110). There is no attempt in our sources to reconstitute an episcopal list before the bishopric of Cyprian (Maier 1973). Thus, it is more likely that there were several Christian organizations in Carthage at the time of Tertullian, organizations that were independent, though sharing a common sense of belonging to the church.

Because Tertullian, in at least one text, clearly includes himself among the clergy (*anim.* 9.4; see Braun 1972: 74), I see no reason to reject the information given by Jerome, and I accept that Tertullian was presbyter. Such status would also have lent him more legitimacy when addressing Christians on pastoral and disciplinary matters, even if his standing as a "sophisticated literate" had, of itself, given him some authority (Tabbernee 2001: 380–381, following Hopkins 1998).

How many Christians were there in Carthage at the time of Tertullian? As with all numbers in antiquity, we can arrive at only a reasonable guess. The population of Carthage in the second century is now estimated at about 70,000 inhabitants (Gros 2000), and Keith Hopkins suggests as a serviceable estimate, though quite likely too high, that Christians composed one-thirtieth of the total urban and metropolitan population of the Empire (1998: 195). If we apply these estimates to Carthage we arrive at a total of fewer than 2,500 Christians in 200 CE.[2] Although this number is very low, perhaps even statistically insignificant, it does not tell the whole story. Indeed, in the pamphlet he addresses to Scapula, the proconsul of Africa, Tertullian warns that persecution of Christians would devastate Carthage, "as everyone would recognize among them relatives and friends" (*Scap.* 5.2). As Timothy Barnes asks, "Could Scapula have confidence that Tertullian was wrong?" (1985: 69). The recent debate about banning the niqab in western Europe similarly shows that a subgroup within a population can become the focus of attention disproportionate to its statistical significance (Scott 2007).

Christian Membership

Definition

First we should consider how Christian membership was defined. Tertullian clearly counts catechumens among the Christians. In the *De corona militis*, he explains that no faithful ever bear a crown and that this is true of all, "from the catechumens to the confessors and martyrs or even the deniers" (*coron.* 2.1). Even if we do not find in Tertullian, as we do in later writers, clear distinctions between the various stages of Christian membership, it seems that Christian membership was broadly understood to start before baptism with admission to the ranks of the catechumens.

Tertullian does not describe how entrance into the ranks of the catechumens was accomplished. He does not mention any specific rite or any sort of screening, but his silence on this matter does not mean that no such rite or screening existed. What seems clear is that there was no fixed catechumenal system, as there would be later on: rules and practices regarding entrance, duration, and instruction probably changed from one organization to another (Saxer 1988: 122–124). Tertullian recommends that baptism not be granted too readily to children and unmarried young people (*bapt.* 18) and insists that it is better to delay baptism than to accept it presumptuously (*paenit.* 6), which confirms, along with the fact that he addresses catechumens in most of his pastoral treatises (*bapt.* 1.1; *paenit.* 6.1; *spect.* 1.1), that he regards them as Christians.

Maintenance

Maintenance of membership does not receive a lot of attention and was probably of no great concern. Tertullian nowhere lists duties that Christians would need to perform in order to remain in good standing. It is true that in the second book of the *Ad uxorem*, for instance, he mentions the "devotions and the duties of the believers" (*fidelium studia et officia*; *uxor.* 2.4.1) that a non-Christian husband might try to prevent his Christian wife from performing: keeping a fast, participating in some charitable expedition, celebrating the Easter vigil, welcoming a foreigner, etc. The performance of these duties would satisfy the Lord according to the requirements of the discipline (*pro disciplina*; *uxor.* 2.4.1). However, Tertullian—who unabashedly sensationalizes the subject to the extent that he portrays all non-Christian men who would marry Christian women as fortune hunters—does not say that failure to perform these duties would jeopardize their Christian membership. Rather, what seems to have been critical was the bishop's recognition of an individual as Christian, which recognition entailed permission to participate in Christian gatherings (Mattei 2007).

Loss

Could Christian membership be lost? The issue is not explicitly discussed. For instance, we have no information about what happened to catechumens who had received several refusals to be admitted to baptism. In the same vein, if a major sin were committed after baptism there was a unique possibility of atonement, the so-called public penance, but Christians who committed a second major sin were not cast out of the Christian organization. It is probable that they simply stayed in the ranks of the penitents for the rest of their lives (Poschmann 1964: 44–49). In the *Apologeticum*, where Tertullian compares Christian membership to memberships more familiar to a non-Christian audience, he seems to imply that sinners were absolutely denied Christian membership (*apol.* 39.4). This is clearly an overly simplistic and apologetic statement, since Tertullian's comments elsewhere, even in the *De pudicitia,* where he holds his most rigorous position on the question of penance, are more nuanced (see Micaelli and Munier 1993: 85–92). In the same passage from the *Apologeticum*, to which I will return, Tertullian also says that there is no "entrance-fee" for Christian membership (*apol.* 39.5).

Rules about Christian membership were seemingly less relevant to the internal life of Tertullian's organization than they were useful for distinguishing it from other organizations that were claiming to be Christian (Mattei 2007). However, because of the nature of our evidence, we can catch glimpses of the everyday Christianity only of the Christians that Tertullian addresses, and it is difficult to evaluate how different this was for the Christians of other organizations.

Expressing Christian Membership

Thus far I have considered how one became and remained a member of a Christian organization. Now I want to ask when and how this membership was made known to outsiders.

External Markers

Shaye Cohen in *The Beginnings of Jewishness* asks the same question about Jews in the Diaspora, and he begins his investigation by appraising a series of external markers: looks, clothing, speech, names, and occupations (1999: 25–68). We can profitably apply a similar appraisal in our own study.

No pagan author attacks Christians for their distinctive looks or speech, and no Christian author complains about such attacks (Labriolle 1934; Benko 1980). Christians in a city like Carthage might have been of Oriental origin, but so were many of the other inhabitants, and this was not enough to distinguish them (Lassère 1977: 406–412).

What about clothing? Tertullian seems to have been sensitive to the importance of clothing as an extension of identity. He notes that Jewish women were distinctive because they wore veils in public (*coron.* 4.2), and that Arabian women even covered their whole face (*virg. vel.* 17.4). Even if these comments are not the result of direct observation—it seems that the evidence on Jewish women derives from the Hebrew Bible (Cohen 1999: 31 and n. 19)—they show that Tertullian was aware of the social (and religious) significance of clothing. This is also confirmed by his polemic tractate on the veiling of virgins, *De virginibus velandis* (see Schultz-Flügel 1997), and by his short piece *De pallio,* in which he encourages—whether seriously or not has long been debated (see more recently Brennan 2008)—Carthaginian men to abandon the traditional Roman toga and to adopt the Greek-style dress of the philosophers, the pallium. However, nowhere does he suggest that Christians wore, or should wear, some distinctive clothing.

While Dionysius, bishop of Alexandria between 248 and 265, notes that Christian children are often named after Peter and Paul (Eusebius Caesariensis, *HE* 7.25.14), no such observations appear in the writings of Tertullian or Cyprian. Because Christian names (on the difficulty of identifying them as such, see Choat 2006: 51–56) disseminated slowly in onomastics (Kajanto 1963; Marrou 1977; Pietri 1977), and because the epigraphic material identified as Christian is of a later date, I will postpone the discussion on names to chapter 3. In the meantime, it can be stated with some certainty that names were not an external marker of Christianity in second- and third-century Carthage (see Rives 1995: 223–224 on the names of the Scillitan martyrs).

As for occupations, some seemed to have been more or less incompatible with Christian membership (see Schöllgen 1982: 3–13 and discussion below), but none were reserved exclusively for Christians. It was therefore impossible to identify a Christian on the basis of his occupation.

In sum, there were no external markers of Christian membership, a situation that Tertullian illustrates in two passages. First, in the *De spectaculis*, Tertullian addresses an imaginary Christian going to the amphitheater to watch a gladiatorial game. He asks: "What will you do if you are caught in the heat of these impious applauses? It's not as if you could suffer anything from men (nobody recognizes you as a Christian), but think about what will happen in heaven" (*spect.* 27.2). There is of course much sarcasm in the rhetorical question. However, the general sense of the message depends on the truth of the assertion that a Christian cannot be identified through external markers. A second passage reinforces this conclusion. In the *Ad Scapulam*, Tertullian states that Christians are "known rather as individuals than as a group," and that they "can be recognized only for the reformation of their former vices" (*Scap.* 2.10). Since the statement is clearly apologetic, we can disregard the opposition between individuals and group. However, individual qualities hardly constitute an external marker, and thus Tertullian confirms that Christian membership could not be determined unless a Christian wished it so.

By Association

Despite the above observations, Timothy Barnes states: "The ordinary Christians of Carthage were a group who could easily be defined and recognized" (1985: 90). Yet this is less at odds with the preceding conclusion than it appears: Barnes goes on to mention Tertullian's affirmation that, unlike heretics and Gnostics, Christians do have fixed meeting places (*praescr.* 42.10). With this observation we are no longer dealing with the possibility of noncontextual external markers that might have identified members of a Christian organization to outsiders; rather, we are recognizing practices that made the members' affiliation known by locating them among other Christians. This is what Shaye Cohen calls "identifying oneself by association" (1999: 53).

Several of Tertullian's texts mention that the Christian organization to which he belongs had a meeting place (White 1996: vol. 2, 54–62). This building has not been identified archaeologically, nor has any location even been proposed for it in Carthage. In fact, it is quite likely that no external architectural features distinguished the building as the meeting place of a Christian organization from one belonging to another religious organization (White 1996: vol. 1, 143–144). Nevertheless, according to Tertullian, the building was known to outsiders and, in particular, to the local and imperial authorities. Thus, in the *Apologeticum*, he writes: "Every day we stand siege; every day we are betrayed; above all in our gatherings and our assemblies we are surprised" (*apol.* 7.4; see *nat.* 1.7.19).[3] This grievance is further developed in the *De fuga persecutionis,* where Tertullian condemns flight and bribery for the sake of avoiding persecution and where he equates apostasy with refusal of martyrdom, since persecution does not happen except with God's consent (Barnes 1985: 178–182). Accordingly, he voices his audience's apprehensions, only to dismiss them: "Since we assemble without order, and assemble at the same time, and flock in large numbers to the church, the pagans make inquiries about us and we fear lest they become agitated about us" (*fug.* 3.4). For Tertullian such fear is simply irrelevant because there will be no persecution unless God wills it. When he deals with bribery and condemns it in all its forms, the problem of gathering appears again: "But how can we assemble, how can we celebrate the Lord's liturgy?" Tertullian's answer is that faith, not bribery, will protect Christians. However, Tertullian concedes: "Lastly, if you cannot assemble by day, you have the night. ... You cannot run through all of the faithful one by one? Be content with a church of three. It is better sometimes not to see your flock than to subject yourselves to bribery" (*fug.* 14. 2). What Tertullian reports as true under the conditions of persecution was very likely true also in ordinary times: to join the Christian gatherings was a clear way of expressing one's membership.

In Tertullian's time there were two types of Christian gatherings in Carthage: a daily morning meeting and a weekly evening meeting (McGowan 2004; Alikin 2010: 93–94, 142–143).[4] The main liturgical event is clearly the weekly evening gathering, called *agape*, which is described most fully in the *Apologeticum*: "Our dinner shows its principle in its name; it is called by the Greek name for love. ... We do not recline until we have first tasted prayer to God. Only so much is eaten as satisfies hunger; only so much drunk as meets the need of the modest. ... After water for the hands come the lights, and then each, from what he knows of the Holy Scripture, or from his own heart, is called before the rest to sing to God as a test of how much he has drunk. Prayer in like manner ends the banquet" (*apol.* 39.16–19). This gathering is essentially a communal meal, a custom common to numerous groups in the Greco-Roman cities, and it probably also included a Eucharistic celebration, though this is not explicitly mentioned (McGowan 2004: 168–169). Additionally, Tertullian makes several allusions to daily meetings at daybreak. Whether the rite of these meetings was the actual celebration of the Eucharist or just the distribution of the bread sanctified during the *agape* is disputed (Alikin 2010: 96–97). This is not especially relevant to our discussion. What is important is the frequency of the Christian gatherings: most other groups that shared a common meal would not have met even once a week, and, for the Christians, a daily meeting before the start of the day's work must have contributed significantly to creating a strong sense of belonging. However, we have no indication of the level of participation, especially at the morning gatherings.[5]

Beyond churchgoing, there were a number of other occasions for a Christian to associate with other Christians. Indeed, in the *Ad uxorem*, Tertullian mentions two types of charitable expedition: feeding martyrs in prison and visiting the poor (*uxor.* 2.4.2). Because of the conditions of imprisonment, it was very common for prisoners to rely on family and friends for their maintenance (Pavón 1999), and this was also true for Christians awaiting trial or execution in prison. A number of texts show that martyrs were visited and fed in prison by other Christians, regardless of whether their family ties had been jeopardized by conversion (McGowan 2003). The *Passio Perpetuae et Felicitatis* describes arrangements made by deacons to assist prisoners (*Passio Perp.* 3.7), while Tertullian alludes to individual initiatives (*mart.* 1.1; *pud.* 22.1; *jejun.* 12). Even if visits to prisoners were common, it seems likely that Christians who fed martyrs were quite easily identified as Christians by the guards and even other visitors because the prisoners they visited were known to be Christians awaiting their trial or execution. Visits to the poor would also have made Christians conspicuous, especially when they were called into areas where they were not expected to be seen. This is clearly what Tertullian has in mind when he describes how uncomfortable a non-Christian husband would be with his wife making such visits: "For who would let his wife, for the sake of visiting the brethren, go round from street to street to others' houses, and especially all around the slums?" (*uxor.* 2.4.2). The common association of Christians with the poor and wretched in pagan attacks ensured that joining a charitable expedition to visit the poor would at least suggest one's identity as a Christian to outsiders (see Groh 1971: 12).

It is sometimes claimed that Christians could also be identified when gathered at their cemeteries. In the *Ad Scapulam*, when Tertullian warns the persecutor of divine vengeance, he evokes, as an example, the episode of 202, when the Carthaginians attacked Christians, violating their tombs: "This is what happened, for example, when Hilarianus was governor: While people were complaining about the grounds where our graves were located, shouting: 'No grounds for them!', it was actually they who lost their grounds; indeed, they did not harvest their grain" (*Scap.* 3.1). The shout "*Areae non sint [Christianis]*" has been interpreted as an indication that Christians had collective and exclusive burial areas (Brandenburg 1994: 212–213; Y. Duval 2000: 448–450). Tertullian also mentions attacks against the tombs of Christians in the *Apologeticum*: "Mad as Bacchanals, they spare not even the Christian dead; no! from the repose of the grave, from what I may call death's asylum, changed as the bodies may be, or mere fragments—they will have them out, rip and rend them" (*apol.* 37.2). But no allusion is made to any reserved space that would naturally attract the attention of a vindictive populace. Rather, Tertullian's reference to the notion of asylum emphasizes that the tombs were attacked in an abandonment of traditional reverence for the quietude of the tomb; for a Roman, there was no greater offense than the violation of the tomb of an enemy. Consequently, as I have shown elsewhere (Rebillard 1996; 2009b: 7–12), there is no need to assume that Christians had collective and exclusive burial grounds in Carthage. Tertullian merely attests here that individual Christians were probably known as such to their neighbors and acquaintances, and that, in case of tensions, their burial plots could be violated.

The impression that Christians were identifiable in their proximate social contexts is also supported by a passage of the *Apologeticum* in which Tertullian mentions those who gossip about the conversion of Christians: "Well, then, what does it mean, when most people shut their eyes and run so blindly into hatred of the Christian name, that, even if they bear favorable testimony to a man, they throw in some detestation of the name? 'A good man,' they say, 'this Caius Seius, except that he is a Christian.' Then another says: 'I am surprised that that wise man, Lucius Titius, has suddenly become a Christian.' ... As sure as a man is reformed by the name, he gives offence. The advantage does not balance the hatred felt for Christians" (*apol.* 3.1). The names, Caius Seius and Lucius Titius, are not only fictive but actually come from law books, where they are used as typical names in stories invented to illustrate a point of law (Lancel 1964). Although Tertullian's point is apologetic—we have already seen his argument for the moral superiority of Christians—it is very likely that an individual's conversion to Christianity gave rise to gossip among his neighbors and acquaintances.

Signs of Identification

I wish to consider briefly two physical gestures that could reveal Christian membership to others. The first is the kiss as a greeting among Christians. Tertullian mentions it as a practice for which a non-Christian husband might fault his Christian wife (*uxor.* 2.4.2). It was common enough that the *Passio Perpetuae* mentions a greeting kiss in the dreams of both Perpetua and Saturus (*Passio Perp.* 10.13 and 12.5). Michael Philip Penn has shown that this greeting kiss functions as a sign of identification, "both to reaffirm membership in the community and as a tool of exclusion" (2005: 59). Though a public greeting kiss was quite common among non-Christians, it was restricted mostly to family and friends (13); the extension of the practice to coreligionists would therefore have distinguished the Christians.

The other gesture was not, like the kiss, a token of membership recognition but could function as an identifier in the eyes of others when performed in public: the gesture of making the sign of the cross on the forehead (Dölger 1958). In the *Ad uxorem*, Tertullian mentions this gesture among other signs through which a Christian wife might betray her religion to her non-Christian husband: "Will you escape notice when you sign your bed or your body?" (*uxor.* 5.1). In the *De corona militis*, he lists all sorts of circumstances and contexts in which a Christian could cross himself: "At every forward step and movement, at every going in and out, when we put on our clothes and shoes, when we bathe, when we sit at the table, when we light the lamps, on couch, on seat, in all the ordinary actions of daily life, we trace upon the forehead the sign [of the cross]" (*coron.* 3.4). That the sign of the cross might have been interpreted as a sign of identification is further suggested in Minucius Felix's *Octavius* where the pagan Caecilianus charges: "They recognize each other by secret marks and signs" (9.2). In his answer, the Christian Octavius simply denies that Christians bear marks on their bodies, and does not elaborate on possible signs of identification, except in a metaphorical way: "We do in fact readily recognize one another, not as you suppose by some token on the body, but by the sign of innocence and modesty" (31.8). The secret (body) mark might be a reference to circumcision, while the signs could be an allusion to the sign of the cross or the use of well-known Christian symbols (Clarke 1974: 214–215).

By Abstention

So far I have considered the positive means by which Christians could reveal their membership to outsiders. Christians could also make themselves conspicuous in a Roman city like Carthage by what they did *not* do and by associations they did *not* maintain. In this section, I will briefly list the circumstances and contexts from which Christians might have been absent, without asking about actual practices, but with an interest in how conspicuous Christian membership would have been on account of their abstentions.

Not every abstention could have been as dramatic as the occasion of the *De corona militis*, when a soldier was condemned to death for holding his garland in his hand rather than wearing it on his head during an imperial donative (*coron.* 1.1). However, Tertullian does dedicate parts of his apologetic treatises to answering accusations made against Christians for their nonparticipation in the life of the cities. In the *Apologeticum*, after discussing accusations of crimes committed in secret, he addresses charges of crimes committed openly (*apol.* 4.2: *in occulto* vs. *palam*; 9.20: *de manifestioribus*): Christians do not worship gods and do not offer sacrifices for the emperors (*apol.* 10.1). Because Tertullian has no intention of denying the first charge—he would, rather, prove that Christians act righteously, because the pagan gods are not gods—he does not explain how exactly abstention from public worship of the gods was reflected in everyday life.

Scholars have traditionally underestimated the capacity of the public cults to attract crowds (MacMullen 1981: 18–34), and, though a number of cults were merely conducted on behalf of the city by priests and magistrates with little if any involvement of the population, it seems that official festivals of the city calendar had an impact on public life (Beard, North, and Price 1998: vol. 1, 259–261). The religious ceremonies that most obviously encouraged popular participation were the *ludi* (games): circus races, theatrical performances, and gladiatorial shows. The *ludi* were performed in association with a religious festival, and sacrifices were publicly performed at their openings (vol. 1, 262–263). However, it is unlikely that failure to attend the games would have counted as abstention from public worship of the gods. More generally, James B. Rives has pointed out that individual participation was not mandatory and not essential, particularly in the Roman tradition (1999: 145–146).[6]

In Carthage, as elsewhere in the Empire, people could also engage in a range of personal religious activities: prayers, offerings, ex-votos, and so on (for Carthage, see Rives 1995: 186–193). It is difficult to say whether Christians' abstention from these activities would have been especially noticeable. The common religious practices of individuals were subject to no oversight, and there were probably few expectations regarding their performance.

Tertullian concludes his reflections on this matter by evoking a situation in which a Christian is compelled to sacrifice and heroically (or stubbornly) holds to his refusal (*apol.* 27.1). I wonder whether accusations of not worshipping the gods were sustained more by early examples of martyrs and common knowledge about Christian beliefs than by any controversy generated by Christians' actual abstention from participation in public worship of the gods.

The second accusation mentioned by Tertullian (*apol.* 10.1) relates to the imperial cult. Sacrifices for the emperors were regularly performed by priests and magistrates, not by the people. On the other hand, from the time of Trajan, the test imposed on Christians at their trial was to perform a sacrifice for the emperor (Pliny, *epist.* 10.96, with Fishwick 1984; see *Passio Perp.* 6.3). In this case too an atypical circumstance, trial for Christianity, is the context of the accusation reported by Tertullian; he does not imply that such an abstention would have singled out Christians in normal circumstances. However, Tertullian also indicates that Christians were accused of not celebrating the holidays of the emperors along with the rest of the population (*solemnia Caesarum*; *apol.* 35.5). A discussion in *De idololatria* about decorating doors with lamps and wreaths on the occasion of an imperial holiday suggests that abstention from this ritual would have marked out the Christian houses quite clearly (*idol.* 15).

Abstention from the religious practices shared by the other inhabitants of Carthage would have singled out Christians. I reserve my discussion of actual practices for later, when we will see that, far from revealing an area of consensus, Tertullian's recommendation to abstain from a given practice usually points to an area of contention among Christians. What I want to note here is that, particularly in a city the size of Carthage, this type of abstention would probably have escaped the attention of the general population, and that it would have been noticeable primarily to neighbors and acquaintances. This is the angle from which I will next approach my inquiry: the interpersonal relations of ordinary social life.

Christianness in Everyday Experience

As we turn to the treatises in which Tertullian describes the social environment as a challenge in the lives of Christians, we shift from a review of identity markers that defined how Christians could be perceived by others to an analysis of how and when Christians perceive their Christianness to be relevant to their identity. As ever, it is important to be alert to rhetorical strategy; I will proceed analytically, paying close attention to the justifications embedded in the objections that Tertullian refutes.

De spectaculis

The first treatise I consider is the *De spectaculis*.[7] Tertullian's goal is to prove that the pleasures of public shows are contrary to Christian faith (*spect.* 1.1). He addresses the treatise both to the baptized and to the catechumens, stating that he wants to eradicate both ignorance and its pretense (1.1). *Ignorantia* and *dissimulatio* are a recurring pair of terms in such treatises (see *cult. fem.* 2.1; *idol.* 2.1; *coron.* 1.6). The rhetorical strategy behind these terms is obvious: positions that contradict Tertullian's definition of Christian faith are not only wrong, but deliberate perversions. To the historian this tactic suggests both that some tension was associated with the issues under discussion, and that Christians justified opposing positions in what they deemed to be Christian terms.

Tertullian's other strategy is to present contrary positions as the opinions of the heathen (*opiniones ethnicorum*; *spect.* 1.3), and thereby to disqualify them automatically. He deals with three such opinions.[8]

The first claims "that pleasures of the eyes and the ears in things external do not hinder religion in the mind and conscience, and that God is not offended by human enjoyment, of which it is no crime to partake, in its proper time and in its proper place, with all due fear and honor secured to God" (*spect.* 1.3). Here Tertullian references not only the putative existence of different spheres, which could be called "sacred" and "secular" (Markus 1990), but also a principle of situational prominence (see above in the introduction), according to which time and place define whether a given membership is relevant. It is not clear how much such a belief owes to paganism. Indeed, Tertullian does not offer a more complete discussion but simply rejects all spectacles collectively.

We can ignore the second argument according to which Christians reject spectacles in order to train themselves for martyrdom, as Tertullian dismisses it as mere slander (*spect.* 1.5), so it holds no value for an investigation into Christian attitudes.

The last argument in this series is attributed to the pagans, but it also seems to have been proposed by Christians. It holds "that all things were created by God and given to man, and that they are really all good, as they are the work of a good creator" (2.1). Tertullian dismisses this as an argument from ignorance, both of the true nature of God, and also of his enemies. It is necessary, rather, "not only to consider by whom all things were created, but also by whom they were perverted" (2.6).

After the "pagan" opinions, Tertullian proceeds to refute an argument that he explicitly attributes to Christians: "There are certain people, of a faith somewhat simple or somewhat fastidious, who seek scriptural authority for the renunciation of public shows and have established doubt in their own minds because abstinence in this matter is not specifically nor in so many words enjoined upon the servants of God" (*spect.* 3.1). Here, as in a number of other places, Tertullian introduces an objection based on what might be called "scriptural legalism": only what is explicitly forbidden in scripture is forbidden to Christians. Tertullian concedes that the circus, the theater, and the gladiatorial games are not mentioned and therefore not forbidden by scripture, but he introduces a principle of exegesis: "Scripture may always be broadly applied wherever discipline is fortified in accordance with the interpretation required by the present circumstances" (3.4). And he goes on to explain how Psalm 1:1 ("Happy is the man who has not gone to the gatherings of the impious, who has not stood in the way of sinners, nor sat in the chair of pestilences") can be applied to the spectacles: "gatherings of the impious" is self-explanatory; "way" (*via*) refers to the alleys of the amphitheaters; "chair" (*cathedra*) designates the seats reserved in the upper part. Tertullian acknowledges that Christians are right to search the scriptures for rules of behavior, but wrong if they will consider only explicit statements. In this particular matter he advocates an allegorizing interpretation that he justifies with recourse to discipline in a somewhat circular manner.[9]

In the second part of the treatise, where he deals with discipline, Tertullian three more times mentions the error of those who accept only specific scriptural rulings. First, he concedes sarcastically that the word *stadium* is in fact mentioned in the scriptures (*spect.* 18.1; see 1 Cor 9:24, for instance). Second, he asks how, after all the proofs he has given, anyone could continue to seek a scriptural condemnation of the amphitheater (*spect.* 19.1). Third, he rejects the search for a direct interdiction in scripture as the desperate maneuver of those who cannot renounce pleasure (20.1). The search for scriptural rulings is mentioned so often that it might be taken for a common practice. However, it should not be forgotten that it was specifically in response to Tertullian's challenges that Christians availed themselves of scripture. We cannot, consequently, assume that scripture was a normal and regular reference in everyday life.

Twice in the *De spectaculis* Tertullian refutes an objection related to the notion of pollution. In the first instance he responds to a possible concern about places (*loca*) associated with idolatry: are they in themselves a source of contamination (*spect.* 8.7–8)? His answer is no, for there is no place in this world that is not in some way or another associated with the demons, and: "For not only the places where men gather for the spectacles, but even the temples themselves, a servant of God can approach without danger to his discipline, provided he has a pressing reason and his reason is unambiguously unconnected with the business or character of the place" (8.8). The principle receives no further elaboration here, but we will encounter a variation of the same argument in the *De idololatria*. The second passage dealing with pollution is Tertullian's mockery of those he calls the *suaviludii* (*spect.* 20; cf. *coron.* 6.3), "the game-lovers": "I heard the other day a novel defense from some game-lover. 'The sun,' he says, 'and even God himself, look on these from the sky and are not defiled.'" Here he adds Diogenes the Cynic's famous aphorism: "The sun sends his rays into the sewer and is not polluted" (Diogenes Laertius 6.63). The targeted *suaviludii* are probably educated Christians,[10] and Tertullian would have been confident that the reference to Diogenes would not go unnoticed. These two objections reveal opposite concerns: one that pollution is inevitable, the other that it is impossible. Concerns about contamination are articulated more explicitly in the *De idololatria*, where Tertullian also provides further indications of his audience's preoccupations.

Of the justifications offered by Christians who see no conflict between their faith and attending the games, two seem genuine. First, when challenged, they counter with scripture's silence on the matter. However, this argument does not imply that they would seek such a warrant even when unchallenged. Our suspicion that this was not, in fact, typical is confirmed by the second justification, according to which there are situations in which faith and Christian discipline are simply not relevant. Two other treatises confirm this picture and introduce new considerations to the discussion.

De cultu feminarum

The *De cultu feminarum* deals with the issues of women's dress and adornment. I have already mentioned Tertullian's awareness of the importance of clothing as an identifier, and his interest in the surfaces and boundaries of the female body has been linked to the challenge of establishing a distinct Christian identity (Calef 1996). Whether one considers the two books of the *De cultu feminarum* as separate works or not, there seems to be a general consensus as to the homiletic nature of the contents of what modern editions give as the second book.[11] Strong evidence of actual delivery invites us to pay close attention to Tertullian's rhetorical strategies, particularly to the objections that he argues against.

At the beginning of his sermon, Tertullian presents what he describes as the most common attitude of women: "Either from simple ignorance or else from bold dissimulation they so conduct themselves as if chastity (*pudicitia*) consisted only in the integrity of the flesh and the avoidance of actual fornication" (*cult. fem.* 2.1.2). He thus acknowledges that Christian women agree that chastity is required by their faith. His contention is that these women have too narrow a conception of what chastity implies. (The same argument is used at the beginning of the *De idololatria* [*idol.* 2.1] regarding the extension [*latitudo*] of idolatry.) We need not specifically address Tertullian's claim that the attitude he denounces is an attempt to limit the requirements of faith on everyday behavior. We should note, rather, that Tertullian's argument provides evidence that these women thought their religion was irrelevant to the way they dressed and adorned themselves.

From several passages, it appears that, when challenged, women used the same stratagem as that which Tertullian attacks in the *De spectaculis*: they asked for scriptural authority. First, he asserts that a scriptural text can be applied beyond its literal meaning. He concedes that makeup is not condemned in the scriptures and ironically suggests: "Let's paint ourselves so that our neighbors may perish!" Developing the topic of neighborly love, he asks: "What then about, 'You shall love your neighbor as yourself' (Mt 19:19), and, 'Care not merely about your own, but about your neighbor's' (1 Cor 10:24)? Enunciation of the Holy Spirit ought to be applied to and concern not only its immediate subject, but also every occasion to which its application is useful" (*cult. fem.* 2.2.5). This is the principle already encountered in the *De spectaculis*. Second, he ridicules the request by providing a text that, read literally, could be used to argue against the dyeing of hair (Mt 5:36: "Which of you can make a white hair black, or out of a black a white?"), and he follows this by sarcastically imagining women who argue with God that they actually dye their hair blond, not white or black (2.6.3). Finally, he alludes to Matthew 6:27 ("Who of you by worrying can add a single cubit to his height?") and derisively applies this verse to sophisticated hair arrangements: "You, however, do add to your weight some kind of rolls, or shield-bosses, to be piled upon your necks!" (2.7.2). To demand scriptural authority before renouncing or adopting any practice is more than a challenge to presbyteral authority: it is a means for Christians to resolve conflicts between their various identities. However, I must insist that we cannot exclude the possibility that conflict exists here only insofar as Tertullian has created it.

Tertullian is well aware that other identities can conflict with Christianness, as is apparent in another passage where he rebukes women who demand scriptural authority: "'Why should we not use what is our own? Who prohibits our using it?' However, it must be in accordance with the apostle, who warns us 'to use this world as if we abuse it not' (1 Cor 7:31). 'For, he says, the fashion of this world is passing away' (1 Cor 10:3)" (*cult. fem.* 2.9.6). Tertullian concedes that some women may be compelled to display their status in public, but he calls for restraint: "Those of you who are compelled by consideration (*ratio*) of wealth, birth, or past dignities to appear in public in such pompous apparel, do make use of moderation in this domain" (2.9.4). Thus, he admits that behavior might be dictated by considerations other than religion. He grants this again when he imagines that women might be concerned about what their social peers would say if they were to change their dressing habits, anticipating the following objection: "Well, but it is urged by some, 'Let not the Name be blasphemed in us, if we make any derogatory change from our old style and dress.'" The answer is again ironical: "This is a grand blasphemy if it is said: 'Ever since she became a Christian, she walks in poorer garb'" (2.11.3). In these two instances, he acknowledges status obligations, while in another passage he accepts that interpersonal relations can also create obligations: "And if the requirements of friendships or duties towards pagans (*necessitas amicitiarum officiorumque gentilicium*) call you, why not go forth clad in your own armor?" (2.11.2). Tertullian's concessions on these points refer to contexts and situations in which Christianness is not necessarily activated by Christian women. The *De idololatria* provides a more thorough review of these.

De idololatria

"*De Idololatria* is a treatise on the practice of Christian life in relation to the (often hidden) religious elements in the heathen world." Such is the description provided by the 1987 editors of the text, Jan Waszink and Jacobus Van Winden (9).[12] It is both true and misleading. True, as far as the treatise deals with practical aspects of the life of Christians. Misleading, as it suggests that the "religious elements in the heathen world," though sometimes hidden, belonged to a well-defined category. In actual fact, Tertullian wrote the treatise specifically because this was not the case, or at least because there was no broad agreement on the issue. As with the other treatises, I am less interested in Tertullian's view than I am concerned with what he reveals about the different and sometimes contradictory attitudes of other Christians.

The subject matter might at first seem quite well delimited: idolatry is the worship of idols. Indeed, Tertullian acknowledges that Christians regard only a limited number of acts as idolatrous: "Most people simply think that idolatry is only then to be assumed, if somebody makes a burnt offering or brings a sacrifice or organizes a sacrificial banquet or makes himself guilty of certain other sacred activities or priesthoods" (*idol.* 2.2). However, he himself defends a much broader understanding of idolatry as the worship of demons, such that "every sin is called *idololatria*, because it is directed against God, and every thing directed against God is in fact a service to the demons" (Van Winden 1982: 113). These claims occasion tensions between Tertullian and his audience and allow us an opportunity to examine the justifications, as he chooses to refute them, that are offered in response to his challenges.

The first part of the treatise deals with questions related to the exercise of occupations. The first case debated is that of idol makers and other artists who are involved in religious activities. After recalling Exodus 20:4 ("You shall make no idol") and a few other scriptural texts (*idol.* 4), Tertullian sets out to refute more specifically the objections raised by artists who seek to become Christian yet do not want to renounce their occupation (5.1). The excuse that they are merely making a living is quickly dismissed, but Tertullian must also reject several scriptural texts presented in favor of the artists' admission to Christianity: 1 Corinthians 7:20 ("As everybody is found, so let him remain"), 1 Thessalonians 4:11 ("Work with your hands, just as we told you"), and Numbers 21:8–9 (where Moses makes a bronze serpent). The extent of disagreement on this issue within the Christian organization is quite impressive. Not only does Tertullian make it clear that there are idol makers among the Christians (when he imagines as a "final argument" the objection of zealous Christians to the defilement that admission of idol makers could cause), but he also reveals that "makers of idols are chosen into the ecclesiastical order" (*idol.* 7.2). After the idol makers, Tertullian also rebukes those artists whose works are pursuant to the worship of idols: painters, marble masons, bronze workers, and so on. Their objections are, as those of the idol makers, related to earning a living. Tertullian proposes that they apply their art to other ends, even if they must receive lesser wages (8). This first series of remarks and objections suggests that some Christians considered occupation an area not relevant to religion. "I make, but I do not worship" is the position they defend (6.2).

Tertullian brings up a second case, astrology, and relates that "the other day somebody challenged [him] by claiming the right to continue this profession" (*idol.* 9.1). We can infer from Tertullian's answer that the astrologer was supporting his claim with Matthew 2:1, the account of the Magi (who first announced Christ's birth), and with the association of magi and astrologers (9.4–6). Again, scriptural authority is invoked.

In his third example, that of schoolmasters, Tertullian makes no reference to an actual case, but he does mention a common objection: "If teaching literature is not permitted to God's servants, learning it will not be allowed either" (*idol.* 10.4). It seems that there were some schoolmasters who did not want to change occupation after their conversion, and also some parents who (lacking the option of an exclusively Christian educational institution) were hesitant to send their children to school. Tertullian's answer is unequivocal: Christian children must go to school, as there is no other way to learn to read and write (10.6), but learning and teaching are two different things. The schoolmaster must inevitably catechize about idols, while the pupil can always reject some of what he learns at school (10.5–6). Although he proposes clear-cut solutions, Tertullian shows that he is well aware of the complexity of negotiating different roles: Christian believer and schoolmaster, Christian believer and parent.

The last occupation considered is trader. Tertullian suggests that the condemnation of covetousness by Paul (1 Tim 6:10) could be cited as scriptural authority for condemning all forms of trade (*idol.* 11.1), before granting that "there exist some righteous forms of gain" (11.2). This debate is illustrated by a specific example: an incense dealer who converted to Christianity but did not want to abandon his occupation. Because incense is so central to the worship of idols (11.3), Tertullian rejects, among other arguments, the justification that incense is also used in medicinal ointment or burnt even by Christians at funerals (11.2).

In the conclusion to the first part of his treatise, Tertullian returns to the objection about the necessity of earning a living. He repeats that this must be taken into consideration before conversion (*idol.* 12.1–4).

These debates illustrate the range of disagreements among Christians, which is a salutary reminder that, in seeking to determine the manner and degree of Christians' participation in the life of their cities, one should not look for a monolithic attitude common to the entire group but rather try to appreciate the range of individual variation. We should also understand that these discussions are not good evidence for Christianity's relevance to the exercise of an occupation: they evince a range of possible responses to issues that arose once it had been made relevant. Indeed, from Tertullian's own testimony, it seems that, for many Christians, including the clergy, occupation was not religiously marked. That Tertullian's focus is selective must be kept in mind.

With a rather weak transition and after reminding us that he had dealt with public games in another treatise, Tertullian defines the topic of the second part of the *De idololatria* as "holidays and other solemnities" or, more generally, "festivities" (*idol.* 12.5–13.1).

The first question is whether a member of the Christian organization should join with non-Christians in their festivities. Tertullian rejects the use of Romans 12:15 ("Rejoice with the rejoicing") as scriptural authorization, thereby attesting that some Christians were citing it when challenged. The next objection is more interesting: "There are certain days on which presents are given. ... Should not I then receive what is my due or pay to another what is due to him?" (*idol.* 13.4–5). Tertullian replies that this custom has been sanctified by superstition (*de superstitione*) and that to participate is therefore idolatry (13.5). He marks as religious a practice that was not necessarily marked as such by other Christians.

Here again we should deconstruct the lines of argumentation that Tertullian imposes on his fictive objectors. The sequence in which he presents the objections need not follow an actual sequence of arguments proposed by Christians. It suffices that the individual objections are plausible and coherent to his audience. Thus the next objection, "that it is pardonable if they [Christians] sometimes do what heathens do, lest the name [of Christianity] be blasphemed" (*idol.* 14.1), implies a fundamental agreement on the religious character of the festivities and offers a justification for participation in spite of this character. However, the appeal to the scriptural authority of 1 Corinthians 10:33 ("just as I also pleased all men in all things") or of 1 Corinthians 5:10 ("otherwise you should have to go out of the world") does not presuppose any such agreement on the religious character of the festivals. Indeed, Tertullian himself reveals that no agreement exists when he mentions that some Christians do celebrate these festivities among themselves (*idol.* 14.6). The festivities included the Saturnalia and the Calends of January, the little-known festival of the Brumae, and the Matronalia (Waszink and Van Winden 1987: 235). Unless we imagine Christians organizing festivities in honor of pagan gods, we must assume that these festivities had no religious character in their eyes but were considered social occasions for rejoicing and gift giving. Hence, when challenged by Tertullian, Christians who did enjoy these celebrations could justify their practice with Romans 12:15, and with the obligation to repay their debts.

The cult of the emperor is also discussed by Tertullian under the topic of holidays and solemnities. He criticizes Christians who, like the heathens, decorate their doors with lamps and wreaths. To the objection that they honor a human being and not a god, Tertullian counters with the theory of euhemerism, according to which all the so-called gods were once human beings (*idol.* 15.2). Christians also cited Matthew 22:21 ("Render to Caesar what is Caesar's") as an objection, for which Tertullian rebukes them with the second half of the verse ("and to God the things that are God's"). He then supplies a further argument: "So you say that the lamps before the doors and the laurel-wreaths at the doorposts are a homage to God?" (*idol.* 15.3–4). Tertullian is, of course, speaking sarcastically. He condemns the decoration of doors as merely a form of idolatry, especially given that pagans, as he notes, worship a whole slew of "door-gods" (15.5). He states clearly that if homage must be paid to emperors it must be within the limits of Christian discipline (15.8–10).

The final arguments regarding festivities concern participation in private celebrations such as betrothals and weddings. Here Tertullian introduces the notion of social duty (*officium*), and in response to the objection "But sacrifices are attached to these solemnities," he says: "Suppose I am invited and the reason for my social duty is not a sacrifice, then the performance of my service can take place as I like" (*idol.* 16.3). The objection could have come from Christians who had reservations about participating in private ceremonies during which a sacrifice was performed, or from those who saw a possible contradiction in the regular participation of Christians in betrothals, weddings, and other familial ceremonies. Regardless, the issue seems to have arisen within a larger discussion about the exercise of an official position in the government of the city or the Empire. Indeed, Tertullian mentions that the topic had recently generated a debate (17.2), in which it seems disagreement was expressed about the possibility of performing official duties without taking part in sacrifice or other acts of idolatry. Tertullian concedes that it is theoretically possible, but expresses strong doubts (17.3). Christians argued from the examples of Joseph and Daniel, who, as Tertullian recalls, served as governors of Egypt and Babylonia respectively. He notes, however, that the comparison is not entirely valid: while the purple worn by Joseph and Daniel in Egypt or Babylonia was a mark of free birth, the insignia of official positions in the Roman Empire are all tainted by idolatry (18.1–3). Moreover, Tertullian adds, "you must know that we cannot always compare things old and new, rude and polished, only just begun and fully developed, servile and free" (18.4). What he points to here is the difference between the Old and the New Testaments: Christ did not exercise any power, and he is *the* model to follow (18.5–7).

Military service prompted similar discussions. Christians who thought that a believer could enroll or a soldier be admitted to baptism called on scriptural examples: "Moses wore a rod (Ex 4:2 and 17:5) and Aaron a buckle (Ex 28:12), John girded himself with a belt (Mt 3:4 and Mk 1:6), Jesus Nave (Joshua) led an army (Ex 19:9), and," Tertullian adds, "Peter waged war (Mt 26:52; Jn 18:11), if I may sport with the matter" (*idol.* 19. 2). I will not expand on the topic of Tertullian's position regarding military service (Schöllgen 1985: 235–239; Waszink and Van Winden 1987: 269–272; more generally, Helgeland 1979). What is of interest here are the dissenting voices, and the general impression that Christians who were prepared to exercise official positions and to accept soldiers into the Christian organization believed that Christianness did not matter in such decisions.

In the final sections of the treatise, Tertullian turns his attention to idolatry in speech (*idol.* 20.1). In his brief introduction, he discusses the meaning of the interdiction of Exodus 23:11, "Make no mention of the names of other gods" (*idol.* 20.3). "Its sense, of course, is not that we should not pronounce their names, which everyday life forces us to use. ... The precept given here is that we do not call them gods" (20.2–3). The examples he provides are interesting: "'You will find him in the temple of Asclepius' or 'I live in the Quarter of Isis' or 'He has become a priest of Jupiter'" (20.2). Indeed, the last example is not neutral: it implies that in everyday life Christians not only had interactions with non-Christians but even expressed interest in the priesthoods their acquaintances held.

Tertullian then deals with oaths in the names of pagan gods. He condemns swearing by Hercules or Medius Fidius, because swearing is a type of oath to these divinities (*idol.* 20.5). He reviews more fully those situations in which Christians may be required to take an oath, and rejects any objection based on what he calls *timiditas*, the fear of being recognized as a Christian (21.1). Tertullian's rhetorical strategy is clear: he presents these objections as a weak (and wrong) apology for what is simply a behavior contrary to Christian faith and discipline. However, we should again bear in mind that, whether or not we suppose these objections were actually argued by some Christians, they are presented in response to Tertullian's challenge, and it need not be assumed that they reflect ordinary cares and concerns.

Indeed, the examples discussed by Tertullian reveal everyday situations in which Christianness was not necessarily relevant for all members of the Christian organization. The first scenario is that of a non-Christian confirming by oath that he will do what he had promised for a Christian (*idol.* 21.1–3). The second is that of a Christian returning a malediction (21.4–5), and here Tertullian presents himself as an eyewitness to such behavior. The third scenario involves a non-Christian blessing a Christian in the name of the gods or in the name of the genius of Carthage (22.1–2). Lastly he addresses the case of a Christian who borrows money and is required to give a guarantee under oath (23.1). Tertullian takes up an initial objection: "I have written, one objects, but I have not said anything; it is the tongue, not the letter which kills" (23.2). This is obviously a reference to some scriptural authority, but no one text matches the citation (Waszink and Van Winden 1987: 288–289). It looks as if it is a conflation of incorrect reminiscences of 2 Corinthians 3:6 ("for the letter kills") and James 3:5–10 (on the evil of the tongue). (Curiously, Tertullian does not note that the scriptural reference is incorrect.) Another objection claims exculpation in the fact that the written document was dictated by the lender (*idol.* 23.3). And a final objection says that "the silent voice of the pen and the mute sound of the letters do not count" (23.5). Tertullian answers with the example of Zacharias, the father of John the Baptist, who was punished by a temporary privation of speech because he did not believe the angel who announced the birth of his son, and regained his voice after he wrote on a tablet the name he chose for his son (Lk 1:20 and 1:62–64). What these exchanges reveal is that such situations were ordinary enough, and that Christians did not routinely activate their Christian membership within them. It is Tertullian who challenges them to do so.

The treatise ends with a brief, uncompromising assertion: to the final objection that idolatry, as Tertullian himself defines it, is impossible to avoid except by leaving the world, Tertullian replies that it is better to leave the world than to live in it as an idolater (*idol.* 24.2).

In my reading of these three treatises, I have tried throughout to resist Tertullian's selective focus on Christianness. When he evokes everyday situations he consistently decontextualizes them in order to force on them his own agenda about what Christianness should entail. However, the numerous objections he feels compelled to refute show that his point of view was not shared, or at least not shared by all Christians. It would be naive to see "real" objections behind all the objections mentioned by Tertullian, but, as I have observed several times, Tertullian's rhetorical strategy could not be effective without somehow relating to his audience's experience.

The picture that emerges from Tertullian's treatises is not solely that of an organization "beginning to experience the problem of conversions at the echelons of middle and borderline upper-class level" (Groh 1976: 47). This conclusion, based on the social composition of the Christian organization (see also Schöllgen 1985), is somewhat reductionist and also adopts Tertullian's point of view when it presupposes a conflict between Christianness and social status. The conflict is of Tertullian's making, and, through the objections he refutes, we can see that Christians activated (or did not according to their individual interpretation of Christianity) the Christian component of their identities in response to circumstance. Such a behavior does not appear to be compatible with the notion that Christians formed a discrete group within their city. It is this question that I explore in the final section of this chapter.

Was There a Separate "Christian World" in Carthage?

The question of whether there was a separate "Christian world" in Carthage is suggested by contemporary ethnicity studies. The production of a separate world can be analyzed both as an ideological project and as a set of social processes. Two main images have been used to describe such separate worlds: that of a parallel world, and that of an enclave nested within the wider world. Whether described as parallel or nested, the idea of a separate world suggests that spheres of life are typically organized into separate segments with variable degrees of enclosure from or interface with the wider world. It also implies a set of institutions through which the members of a separate world can satisfy their needs, which usually include education, work, food and clothing, and social assistance (see Brubaker et al. 2006: 265–269 with further references).

We have already seen that the Christian organization did not operate a separate school system. In the *De idololatria*, Tertullian admits that Christians must necessarily receive instruction in the secular institutions (*idol.* 10, on which see above; Schöllgen 1982: 11–12; 1985: 231–232), and his injunction against members of the Christian organization working as teachers seems to have been quite idiosyncratic (Berardino 1972). In none of his denunciations of various occupations does Tertullian suggest that to work for the Christian organization or for another of its members could, or should, constitute an alternative. In the *Apologeticum*, he refutes the accusation that Christians are unprofitable in business: "How can this be true of men who live with you [non-Christians], who enjoy the same food, clothes, and furniture, same necessities of life? . . . Consequently we cannot dwell together with you in the world, without your forum, without your meat market, without your baths, shops, factories, taverns, fairs, and other places of business" (*apol.* 42.1–2). Even "idol-meat," that is, meat offered in sacrifice to idols, which was regularly sold at the meat market, does not seem to have been banned from the tables of Christians (Rebillard 2010).

So far there is not much evidence for the existence of a separate Christian world. However, one area remains to be explored: social assistance. In the *Ad uxorem*, Tertullian mentions the charitable expeditions that a non-Christian husband might prevent his Christian wife from joining (*uxor.* 2.4.2; see above). He also notes that in a mixed marriage it would be difficult for a Christian wife to welcome a Christian foreigner into her house. In the *De idololatria*, when he rebukes Christians who agree to sign loan contracts that include a guarantee under oath (see above), Tertullian suggests looking to other Christians for assistance as an alternative: "Let us pray the Lord that the necessity for such a contract may never come over us and that, if such a thing should happen, He may confer on our brethren the means for helping" (*idol.* 23.7).

The extant text in which Tertullian most fully describes Christian social assistance is the *Apologeticum*, where he compares the Christian organization to an association (*corpus*). There he explains that each member donates money according to his means, which is then used "to feed the poor and to bury them, for boys and girls who lack property and parents, and then for slaves grown old, for shipwrecked persons, and for any who may be in mines, islands, or prisons, provided that it is for the sake of God's school, and they thus become pensioners of their confession" (*apol.* 39.6). Before looking at the importance of the assistance offered to its members by the Christian organization, I should clarify what Tertullian means by the comparison with an association.

There is no longer any need to refute the hypothesis of Giovanni Battista De Rossi (or its more recent avatars), according to which Christian organizations adopted the legal status of funerary associations (Rebillard 2009b: 42–47). The extent to which the analogy with Greco-Roman associations is useful for reconstructing the character of early Christian organizations is another question altogether. When Tertullian points to common features such as regular meetings, the office of president, or the collection of money, he does so only to emphasize the differences: Christians meet to pray, not for banquets; honorary positions cannot be bought; the money collected is not used for the contributors, but for the poor, widows, and orphans (*apol.* 39; see Waltzing 1912 for a detailed analysis). Despite interesting insights arising from the analogy (see Harland 2003, 2009), it cannot be pushed too far, and we cannot assume that Christians considered their Christian membership to exclude memberships in one or more of their city's associations (see Rebillard 2009b: 50–56). In any case, the analogy as it is understood now, in light of recent scholarship on Greco-Roman associations, does not point to a separate world, but to higher levels of integration within local society (Harland 2009).

The beneficiaries of assistance for the poor—widows, orphans, aging slaves, and shipwrecked mariners—were clearly all Christians, while assistance for imprisoned or exiled Christians was restricted to those who suffered on account of their faith. The extent of assistance might have been limited, but it undeniably contributed to the creation of a bounded group. However, despite offering these forms of charitable assistance, the Christian organization of Tertullian did not form or maintain institutions that could create a separate Christian world. I have already mentioned that there is no solid foundation for the hypothesis that separate burial grounds existed for Christians. David Hunter (2003) has recently shown that there were no specific rites for marriage, and Tertullian's works clearly attest to the fact that Christians did intermarry with non-Christians (Schöllgen 1982: 23–27).

To conclude that there was no separate Christian world is not to deny the existence of a sense of common identity, clearly attested, for instance, by the use of familial language to refer to fellow members (*apol.* 39.7; see Pétré 1948: 118–124) and further enforced by the frequency of their meetings.[13] However, Christianness was only one of the many affiliations that mattered in everyday life, and we should not assume that the degree of groupness associated with the Christian category was as high, stable, and consistent as Tertullian claims it should be. We need therefore to take into consideration that Christians, as the other inhabitants of the Roman Empire, did not belong to only one collectivity that determined their identity. The next chapter will focus on the limits of religious allegiance in the context of episodes of persecution between the end of the second and the beginning of the fourth century.

CHAPTER 2

Persecution and the Limits of Religious Allegiance

In the *Historia ecclesiastica*, Eusebius describes a succession of periods of persecution and periods of peace corresponding to the reigns of different emperors. However, Eusebius's view of these events is skewed by his contemporary circumstances, and his narrative of the persecutions is, as a result, distorted by a number of erroneous assumptions (Barnes 1985: 149). There is now general agreement among historians that before the reign of Decius there was no imperial legislation against the Christians (De Ste. Croix 1963; Barnes 1968),[1] and that Decius himself did not even have the Christians in mind when he issued his edict (Rives 1999). Rather, persecution was a local matter, ultimately in the hands of the governors. In most cases, Christians were denounced to the authorities and arrested—it was a crime to be a Christian[2]—and then tried by the governor. Christians could be denounced either individually or in groups. Evidence on the denunciations themselves is scarce beyond the mention of the *delator*, usually identified as the devil (Rivière 2002: 318), and consequently it is difficult to determine exactly why Christians were denounced. This is also all the more reason to proceed with care and to resist uncritical acceptance of the usual claims about popular hatred.[3]

I will review episodes of persecution in North Africa from the end of the second century until the beginning of the fourth. North African documentation, which is particularly abundant and has been thoroughly studied,[4] will allow us not only to measure the intensity of the persecutions, and therefore the level of threat that they implied for the everyday life of Christians, but also to analyze how the category "Christians" was used in these contexts and by whom. While revisiting the evidence on the behavior of Christians, as individuals and as a group, I will also try to determine the mechanisms of Christian mobilization in response to persecution.

Persecutions in the Time of Tertullian

In the final section of his own review of the evidence, Timothy Barnes draws two conclusions: on the one hand, the number of executed Christians must have been "comparatively small," as no African bishop died as a martyr before Cyprian in 258 (Pontius, *V. Cypr.* 19; Barnes 1985: 162); on the other hand, even if persecution was sporadic, "Christians could never feel permanently safe" (161). The question of the number of executed Christians is difficult,[5] but the exact number is not so important in my view—even a handful of martyrs could have been sufficient to foster a sense of groupness among Christians. It is more crucial to evaluate how heavily the threat of persecution weighed on everyday life. Thanks to the detailed prosopographical studies of Anthony Birley (1991, 1992), we can now quite precisely reconstruct the chronology of the episodes of persecution in North Africa.

Episodes of Persecution before 197

In the *Ad Scapulam*, Tertullian reports that Vigellius Saturninus was the first proconsul to put Christians to death in North Africa (*Scap.* 3.4). The date of Saturninus's African proconsulship, 180–181, provided by the *Acts of the Scillitan Martyrs*, fits with what is known of his career from inscriptions (Birley 1992: 37–38), and it is usually assumed that Tertullian refers to the Scillitan martyrs, although he does not mentioned them explicitly. The *Acts* themselves start in medias res during Saturninus's hearing of the Christians, and the Scillitan origin of the martyrs is only known through later tradition (Ruggiero 1991: 48–49). The *Acts* contain no mention of the circumstances of the arrest of the Christians, nor is anything reported about their relationships to one another. Most of the text is dedicated to the interrogation of Speratus, who is sometimes deemed to be the "spokesman" of the group (Ruggiero 1991: 50). Indeed, the text itself seems to single out Speratus from the rest of the group (*ceteris*; *Scill.* 7) and reports that all the other Christians approved his decision to decline the offer of a thirty-day delay to consider their testimony (13). Speratus also carries a book of the scriptures with him:

some letters of Paul (12). If we accept Hopkins's (1998) speculation that the number of literate Christians was small, then Speratus's status was certainly exceptional. It seems probable that this group of Christians—whether they were six or twelve is an unsolvable question (Ruggiero 1988)—was arrested during a regular gathering. This is consistent with Tertullian's complaint about harassment during daily meetings (*apol.* 7.4; see chapter 1).

The Scillitan martyrs may not have been the first Christians to be brought before a governor. Tertullian, in a list of four governors who decided not to prosecute Christians, mentions Vespronius Candidus (*Scap.* 4.3), who is known to have been the legate of the III Augusta based in Lambaesis, Numidia, between 174 and 176, and in this capacity he can be considered de facto governor of Numidia (Birley 1992: 44). If it was in this capacity that Candidus heard the case, the hearing then necessarily predated the martyrdom of the Scillitan Christians by several years.[6] Tertullian says that Candidus sent a Christian back home, after he had condemned him as a disturber so as to satisfy the citizenry (*Scap.* 4.3). Here, there is a clear indication of the reason the Christian found himself before the governor: his fellow citizens denounced him. However, their motives are not reported.

The next episode reported by Tertullian involves Cingius Severus,[7] whose proconsulship is known only from Tertullian and is tentatively dated to 195–196 or 196–197 (Birley 1992: 44 n. 52). Cingius Severus heard Christians in Thysdrus and allowed them an opportunity to be released without apostasy (*Scap.* 4.3). This case confirms that local initiatives were not always pursued by the governor. However, the Christians were probably arrested and held in prison for some time.

Thus it appears that, between 180 and 197, only scattered incidents of persecution occurred in North Africa, or at least so far as Tertullian knew; his narratives of this period are hardly saturated with Christian bloodshed.[8]

The Years 197 and 198

The years 197 and 198 were marked by more dramatic incidents. The proconsul for 197–198, whose name is not known, did not share the attitude of his predecessor Cingius Severus. When Tertullian wrote the *Ad martyras*, probably in the summer of 197, some Christians were in prison awaiting execution. He calls them *benedicti martyres designati* (*mart.* 1), which suggests that they had already been tried and condemned to death. A few months later, when he wrote the *Apologeticum*, several Christians had already been put to death, and Tertullian graphically describes the tortures they suffered (*apol.* 12.3–5, 21.28, 30.7, 49.3, 50.3–12).[9]

Although the *Apologeticum* is addressed to Roman magistrates in general, Tertullian makes it clear that the treatise is written specifically in reaction to recent events when he recalls that "recently" during a trial Christians were denied the right to defend themselves (*proxime*; *apol.* 1.1). The adverb is used again twice. At the end of the treatise, Tertullian refers to another incident: "For quite recently by condemning a Christian woman to the lust of man rather than to a lion, you confessed that the stain upon chastity is reckoned more heinous among us than any punishment and any death" (50.12). More interesting is the anecdote he recounts after he has refuted the claim that the Christian God has an ass's head: "Quite recently in this city a new representation of our god has been displayed, since a certain person, a criminal hired to dodge wild beasts in the arena, exhibited a picture with this inscription: 'The God of the Christians, ass-begotten'. It had ass's ears; one foot was a hoof; it carried a book and wore a toga" (16.12). He reports the same story in the contemporary treatise, the *Ad nationes*, where he adds that the culprit was a Jewish apostate (*nat.* 1.14). As Claude Aziza (1974) has argued, we need not suppose that the Jews were in fact responsible for this caricature of the Christian God. In the *Apologeticum*, Tertullian does not even mention that the man is of Jewish origin. This anecdote does illustrate how Christians could be ascribed a collective (and negative) identity. Nevertheless, if the Christians in Carthage were stigmatized as a group, it does not necessarily follow that they perceived themselves as such in their everyday life.

The denunciation of popular hatred is unquestionably a leitmotif in the *Apologeticum* (2.3, 4.1, 40.1). Tertullian goes so far as to complain that Christians are blamed for every public disaster: "If the Tiber rises to the walls, if the Nile does not rise to the fields, if the sky is rainless, if there is an earthquake, a famine, a plague, immediately the cry arises, 'The Christians to the lion!'" (*apol.* 40.1). According to Tertullian, the populace not only perceives the Christians as a group, but they also carry out attacks against the group thus construed. He reports acts of violence, for instance: "How often also, bypassing you [Roman magistrates], does the hostile mob of its own right attack us with stones and fires? With the very rage of Bacchanals, they do not spare Christians even when they are dead. No! From the rest of the tomb, from the sort of refuge that death affords, they would drag them away, cut them up, tear them to pieces, when they are already decomposed, when they are already not even entire" (37.2). Even if, as I have contended elsewhere (Rebillard 2009b: 7–12), we need not imagine pagans attacking Christian communal cemeteries, we see here that the Carthaginian population, or at least some elements in it, perceived the Christians as a group and attacked them as such. However, we have little evidence about how Christians reacted to these attacks.

Tertullian clearly suggests that in these circumstances Christians constituted a bonded group, and thus positioned themselves. This is what is intended by the famous "The blood of Christians is seed" (*apol.* 50.13). However, we will see that, even according to Tertullian himself, the situation on the ground was not always so clear-cut.

Anthony Birley has suggested that "persecution in the years from 197 to 198 might well have been sparked, in North Africa not least, by the purges which followed the defeat of Severus' rival Clodius Albinus at Lugdunum in February 197" (1992: 41). Indeed, in the three treatises written on the events of these years Tertullian makes several references to the political climate and in particular explicitly defends Christians against accusations of treason (*mart.* 6.2; *nat.* 1.17.4; *apol.* 35, with Barnes 1985: 32–34). It is worth noting that "popular" attacks against Christians happened precisely in the context of political purges. Even if Christians were undeniably used as scapegoats, the reasons why the *populus* sought scapegoats in the first place might have had nothing to do with religious affiliation. The local situation was particularly tense as Clodius Albinus, who himself came from Hadrumetum in Proconsular Africa, had many supporters there (Birley 1992: 41 nn. 32 and 33). In the end, "persecution" in this case could have been a means for the authorities to deflect attention from acts of political retaliation, rather than a symptom that "the pagan mob" was "a bitter and implacable foe" of the Christians (Barnes 1985: 159).[10]

Hilarianus the Persecutor (202–203)

We have no evidence that there were trials of Christians in Carthage between 198 and 202, when P. Aelius Hilarianus was made acting governor in place of Minucius Opimianus (Birley 1992: 46). Hilarianus sentenced the famous Perpetua and her companions to be sent to the beasts during the celebration of the birthday of Septimius Severus's son Geta, on March 7, 203.[11] James Rives (1996) has made a thorough examination of Hilarianus's motivations. Both his decision to accept the charge against the Christians, and the harsh punishment he inflicted on them indicate that he viewed Christianity as a serious problem. This is corroborated by further evidence of his religious conservatism.

There is no evidence on how the case of Perpetua and her companions was brought to Hilarianus's attention. In the *Ad Scapulam*, Tertullian mentions popular anti-Christian agitation at the time: "Under the governor Hilarianus, they shouted about our tombs: 'No grounds for them!' It was actually they who lost their grounds: indeed they did not harvest their grain" (*Scap.* 3.1). (We note in passing that Tertullian here again suggests that Christians are ascribed a collective identity by the population.) Anne Daguet-Gagey has suggested that the celebration of the Decennalia of Septimius Severus in 202 created a situation in which Christians by their abstention might have caused some resentment (2001: 24–25). As we saw in chapter 1, it is not clear how such abstention could have been noticeable, and it is not obviously the case that a majority of Christians would in fact have abstained from participation.

James Rives points out that there is "no reason to think that Hilarianus was under extreme pressure from the populace" and notes that the crowd accordingly plays a relatively limited role in the *Passion* (1996: 23). In the few instances where the crowd is mentioned, its role is even more ambivalent than acknowledged by Rives. A huge crowd attends the trial but is totally passive (*Passio Perp.* 6.1). However, during the execution, reactions are mixed: the people are enraged when the martyrs seem to threaten them (18.9), compassionate when the two young women are brought naked into the arena (20.2–3), but show no pity and even excitement when it comes to the final execution (21.2 and 7).[12] However, these details must be viewed within the economy of the text itself, and it seems rather hazardous to ground an evaluation of Hilarianus's attitude on them.

Whatever its source and motives, the denunciation seems to have targeted a small, specific group of recent converts. They were all catechumens and young (*Passio Perp.* 2.1). Felicitas and Revocatus were slaves, but we know nothing of the status of Saturninus, Secundulus, and Saturus. Perpetua herself is usually thought to be from a family of good standing, a member of the decurial class, if not of senatorial rank (Schöllgen 1985: 197–202; but see Cooper 2011: 688–690 for a revisionist position). It is commonly supposed that the martyrs all belonged to a single household (see Barnes 1985: 72), but nothing in the circumstances of their arrest either supports or contradicts this assumption. According to the *Passion*, they were all arrested at the same time, while they were meeting, except Saturus, their instructor, who was absent and later self-surrendered (*Passio Perp.* 4.5). It seems that Perpetua and her companions were arrested in the small city of Thuburbo Minus, rather than in Carthage, but no clear account is given of their transfer to Carthage, where they were tried and executed (Amat 1996: 22–25).

The *Passion* does mention a few other Christians, in particular two deacons, Tertius and Pomponius, who take care of the martyrs while they are in prison (*Passio Perp.* 3.7, 6.7). The only other visitors mentioned are family members of Perpetua, whose mother was probably Christian herself, as was one of her two brothers.[13] However, it is as family members that they visit

Perpetua, not as fellow Christians. Indeed, the *Passion* gives no indication of other Christians' feelings about the events.

The only trial reported to take place under Hilarianus was that of the *Passion*. No doubt, as emphasized by Rives, Hilarianus's personal hostility to Christianity played a role in his decision to accept the case and in the way he conducted the trial. He might also have seen the trial as an opportunity to provide an extraordinary spectacle for the celebration of the birthday of Septimius Severus's son Geta. As mentioned above, Tertullian attests to some popular exactions levied against Christians under Hilarianus's magistracy (*Scap.* 3.1), but on the whole the martyrdom of Perpetua and her companions seems to have been an isolated episode.[14] The execution of Guden (which took place three months later in June 203, if we are to believe a list of martyrs compiled in the ninth century) is unrelated.[15]

The Executions of 212–213

In the *De corona militis*, Tertullian mentions "a good and long period of peace" (*coron.* 1.5). This period of peace has traditionally been interpreted as the period between 203 and 211 (see, for instance, Fontaine 1966: 51), when Tertullian reports the execution of a Christian soldier (Le Bohec 1992: 12 for the dating). The rebellion of this soldier is also traditionally deemed to have sparked the persecution in 212 (see, for instance, Freudenberger 1970: 579). However, it has been convincingly argued that the soldier's execution took place in Rome rather than in North Africa (Le Bohec 1992; Y. Duval 1995: 31–32). Thus the affair does not concern the events of the years 212 and 213 in Carthage.

On the other hand, "peace" in this context means, at best, no executions; we happen to know that charges against Christians were brought before the proconsuls in 209–210 and 210–211, whom Tertullian lists among the governors favorably inclined toward Christians in the *Ad Scapulam*. The first of these is C. Julius Asper, whose proconsulship has recently been dated to 209–210 (Dietz 1997; see Birley 2005: 181–183). Asper "had a man mildly punished and at once sent away without compelling him to make sacrifice—having previously avowed, in front of lawyers and assessors, his regret that he himself had landed in a case of this kind for the first time" (*Scap.* 4.3). As Barnes points out, the fact that Asper attained the position of proconsul without ever having previously tried a Christian implies that trials of Christians were not especially frequent (1985: 162). The second governor mentioned is C. Valerius Pudens, who was probably in office in 210–211 or 211–212 (Birley 1992: 45). Tertullian says "that Pudens too released a

Christian who had been sent to him when he understood that the accusation involved extortion, and that he tore apart the accusation before declaring that, in accordance with the law, he would not hear a case against a man with no accuser" (*Scap.* 4.3). Here is attested a case of the "secondary motives" (Lane Fox 1987: 425) that must have been the underlying causes of at least some of the denunciations of Christians.

When Tertullian wrote his treatise addressed to Scapula—probably C. Julius (Scapula) Lepidus Tertullus, who might have been Carthaginian (Birley 1991: 80–81 n. 1; 1992: 53)—soon after an eclipse datable to August 14, 212, Scapula had already tried and tortured several Christians (*Scap.* 4.2),[16] and likewise his colleagues in Numidia and Mauretania (4.8). Tertullian does not provide any details of the trials or of how the charges were presented to the governors. However, he insinuates Scapula's accountability when he implies that, after the attitude of the governor toward the Christians became known, abuses by soldiers and denunciations by envious individuals multiplied: "Spare the province, which the indication of your purpose has subjected to the extortions of soldiers and private enemies" (5.3). Anthony Birley suggests that the political atmosphere of 212 might explain the outburst of persecutions, as had been the case in 197–198 (Birley 1992: 53). There was a massive purge in Rome after the murder of Geta in December 211 (Meckler 1994: 130–131). Although no evidence exists that the purge was extended to the provinces, and to North Africa in particular, the possibility cannot be ruled out.

In his pamphlet, Tertullian warns Scapula of the unfortunate consequences that persecuting Christians would entail for him. He thus evokes the miserable fate of some persecutors (*Scap.* 3), and he also threatens the governor with a form of collective action. He recalls that, when the proconsul of Asia, Arrius Antoninus, began to hold trials against Christians, all the Christians of the region presented themselves at his tribunals as a group (*manu facta*; *Scap.* 5.1). As to the potential consequences of such a move in Carthage: "If we decide to do this here too, what will you do about thousands of people, men and women, of every sex and every age and every rank when they present themselves to you? How many fires, how many swords will you need? How will Carthage itself tolerate decimation at your hands when each man knows relatives and friends there?" (5.2). Most commentators have referred this threat to Tertullian's tendency to exaggeration and added it to the dossier of voluntary martyrdom (Lane Fox 1987: 442; Bowersock 1995: 1–3; De Ste. Croix 2006: 167), while Oliver Nicholson has recently suggested that such a passage evinces strategic thinking on the part of the church (2009: 71–73). I think the passage needs to be contrasted with Tertullian's statement earlier in the same treatise: "Though our numbers are so great—constituting all but the majority in every city—we conduct ourselves so quietly and modestly, known perhaps one by one rather than all at once, and remarkable only for the reformation of our former vices" (*Scap.* 2.10). Here Tertullian reveals that the governor would hardly realize how numerous Christians are, precisely because they do not act as a group. My point is not merely that Tertullian contradicted himself to suit his rhetorical needs, at one moment warning the governor of an invisible multitude, and at another threatening him with the necessity of open confrontation with the Christians en masse. I want to suggest that Tertullian probably wished that such a collective action were possible, but in the light of what he says of the behavior of Christians in times of persecution it does not seem very likely.

Conclusion

From the record of the persecutions, as Tertullian strove to construct it for his fellow Christians, we see that persecution was not so constant a threat as is typically assumed. Tertullian records one or two executions before 197 (the six or twelve Scillitan martyrs and Mavilus), and he is direct witness to persecutions in 197–198, 202–203, and 212–213. Over sixteen years, therefore, executions of Christians are attested during three periods, each of which lasted only a few months and that were separated respectively by four years (between 198 and 202) and nine years (between 203 and 212). Of course, the absence of executions does not mean that there were no denunciations, and Tertullian attests to these when he mentions governors who did not follow up on local denunciations. However, even denunciations seem to have been too sporadic to constitute a permanent threat.[17]

Neither Tertullian nor the North African *Acts of Martyrs* records any cases of denunciation brought before a governor as having originated in Carthage; it is as if denunciations by neighbors, family, or friends were less likely to arise in a large city.[18] On the other hand, Tertullian implies that the initial reaction of a governor to such denunciations could have a snowball effect in his province (see above, *Scap.* 5.3). One is tempted to suppose that this might explain why, with the exception of the few cases of individual denunciations to governors reported by Tertullian, it was usually groups of Christians who were prosecuted.

Because of the crucial role of denunciations in the persecutions of Christians until the mid-third century, historians have concluded that they were largely the result of public odium (Barnes 1968: 48, 50; 1985: 158 for North Africa; Engberg 2007 for an attempt at a more systematic examination).

Popular animosity and resentment are usually explained as reactions to the antisocial attitude of the Christians (see, for instance, De Vos 2000), but this does not fit well with the picture drawn in chapter 1. In fact, it appears that both popular hatred and the antisocial attitude of the Christians are a construct of the same texts. Tertullian tries to mobilize Christians by emphasizing the communal hostility of the pagans, as do the *Acts of Martyrs*: the *delator* is conspicuously absent in the narratives of the *Acts*, but the crowd is a regular actor, underlining the collective dimension of the hostility Christians face. Whether or not the non-Christian populace was actually united in communal hostility to Christians is probably impossible to establish.[19] We will look instead for evidence of communal response on the part of the Christians.

Tertullian and the Mobilization of Christians during Persecution

I will now consider whether Tertullian succeeded in mobilizing Carthaginian Christians facing persecution, and what strategies he used in striving to do so. Here, Tertullian's attitude to martyrdom (see Barnes 1985: 164–186; and Bähnk 2001 for a recent treatment) is of less interest than what his treatises reveal about the behavior of Christians, and about the forces, both centrifugal and centripetal,[20] that influenced the church.

Ad martyras

The only treatise written in the heat of a persecution and addressed to Christians in prison awaiting trial and martyrdom is the *Ad martyras* (on its dating to 197, see above). As René Braun has masterfully demonstrated, this short text follows the structure of a letter of exhortation. It is divided into two parts, the first describing the present evils of prison, and the second concerning the future evils of death (Braun 1978). The fact that Tertullian wrote and circulated this letter of exhortation can be construed as a form of communal response. The same is true with the food provided to the martyrs in prison. Twice Tertullian mentions that the prisoners are provided with food thanks to the help of their "brothers" (*mart.* 1.1, 2.7). Such support is corroborated by other evidence (see McGowan 2003; also chapter 1 above) and clearly attests to a form of communal response, albeit a rather passive one.

De corona militis

Though the martyrdom of the Christian soldier is not relevant to the history of North African Christianity (see above), Tertullian's reactions to the incident are germane.[21] Tertullian wrote the *De corona militis* because some Christians did not approve of the behavior of the soldier who refused to wear a crown and so disclosed himself as Christian: "Thereafter adverse judgments began to be passed upon his conduct—whether on the part of Christians I do not know, for those of the heathen are not different—as if he were headstrong and rash, and too eager to die, because, in being taken to task about a mere matter of dress, he brought trouble on the bearers of the name, as if he alone were brave among so many soldier-brethren, he alone a Christian" (*coron*. 1.4). It seems that Carthaginian Christians disagreed about the propriety of the soldier's attitude: the pro–New Prophecy Christians praised his behavior, while "mainstream" Christians did not (see *coron*. 1.4, with Fontaine 1966: 50, and now Tabbernee 2007: 232–234). Thus, far from necessarily engendering groupness, martyrdom could actually nurture divisions among Christians.

Scorpiace

It is generally agreed that the *Scorpiace* shows no evidence of Montanism, but Barnes's proposed dating to 203 (1969; 1985: 34–35, 328–329) has not been widely accepted (see Braun 1972: 79–80). The alternative hypothesis of a logical development that would place the writing of *Scorpiace* between the *De corona* and the *De fuga*, and thus in 212, is equally tenuous (Azzali Bernardelli 1990a).

Tertullian wrote the *Scorpiace* to discourage his fellow Christians from evading persecution.[22] He makes it clear that Christians have already been tried and executed: "And now we are in the midst of an intense heat. ... Christians have been put to the test: some by the fire, others by the sword, others by the beasts" (*scorp*. 1.10–11; see 9.12). He describes the Christians' morale in these circumstances: "The hot season for Christians is persecution. When, therefore, faith sweats with anxiety and the Church, as the burning bush, is consumed by the flames, then the Gnostics break out, then the Valentinians creep forth, then all the opponents of martyrdom bubble up, being themselves also hot to strike, pierce, kill. For, because they know that many Christians are simple and also inexperienced, and weak moreover, that most in truth swerve with the wind and are Christians when it suits them, they perceive that it is best to approach them when fear has opened the entrances to the soul, especially when some display of ferocity has already crowned the faith of the martyrs" (*scorp*. 1.5). Tertullian suggests that persecution provoked defections in the ranks of the Christians. Clearly some were unwilling to bear witness once executions had begun, and Tertullian stigmatizes them as simple and ignorant, easy prey for heretics. Tertullian also rejects the possibility of denying being Christian without denying Christ himself (9.9–13), thus suggesting that some Christians thought that this was possible. These Christians meant not to abandon their membership in the Christian organization, but simply to lie about it to the authorities. In his discussion, Tertullian recalls that during recent trials, Christians were not only asked to deny their Christianity, but also to curse Christ (9.12).

I leave open the question of whether Tertullian witnessed Valentinian or other Gnostic proselytism.[23] It was in any case compelling for Tertullian to present Christians as heretics if they believed that martyrdom might be evaded without violating the requirements of membership in the Christian organization, and Valentinian doctrine is here deployed merely to bolster his argument.

Even as Tertullian attests to defections under the duress of persecution, he also indicates how the Christian organization tried to construct a communal response by rejecting as "heretics" those Christians who did not stand firm but chose instead to deny their membership. It is simply impossible to evaluate how successful such a strategy might have been in stopping defections, but it must have effected at least a tightening of the ranks of the faithful.

De fuga in persecutione

Interest in the *De fuga in persecutione* has mainly focused on Tertullian's position on flight from persecution and its evolution under the influence of Montanism (see Barnes 1985: 176–183; Tabbernee 2007: 244–253; more generally on flight from persecution, see Nicholson 1989).[24] However, the text is also interesting for the testimony it offers on the centrifugal pressures exerted on Christian organizations. Tertullian wrote the treatise for an acquaintance of his, called Fabius, who is otherwise unknown. Some impending threat gave rise to Fabius's question regarding the correct response when faced with persecution, and at the time of writing persecution was ongoing (*fug.* 1.1, 1.3).

Tertullian's first point is that persecution arises by the will of God and for his glory. To prove his point he explains that persecution generates fear and that fear strengthens faith: "When is faith in God stronger than when there is greater fear of him, than during persecution? The church is stunned. Then is faith both more zealous in preparation, and better disciplined in fasts, and meetings, and prayers, and lowliness, in brotherly-kindness and love, in holiness and temperance" (*fug.* 1.6–7). Again, we see here how Tertullian encourages a communal response to persecution and tries to reinforce group cohesion. The picture he draws should not be taken at face value, however, as it is clearly contradicted by the tone and content of the rest of the treatise. Thus some Christians are willing to stop attending the liturgical meetings for fear of being caught: "As we assemble without order, and assemble at the same time, and flock in large numbers to the church, the pagans make inquiries about us and we fear lest they become agitated about us" (3.4). Far from displaying the better discipline desired by Tertullian, these Christians suggest that they are not willing to denounce themselves by participating in Christian gatherings.

In the rest of the treatise, Tertullian uncompromisingly condemns both flight and bribery as forms of apostasy. It is impossible to evaluate the number of Christians who chose one of these two options rather than face trial and death. Both required financial means, and thus were not affordable to everybody. But it is quite obvious that those who chose to flee or to bribe officials thought it compatible with their faith. Accordingly, Tertullian evokes and refutes several objections based on scriptures. There is, furthermore, no suggestion in Tertullian's writing that, after a period of persecution, Christians who had fled or used bribery must be reconciled before resuming their membership. Tertullian's attitude has been described as extreme and attributed to his "Montanism" at the time these treatises were written. His opinion, clearly, is not shared by the majority in the Christian organization he belongs to, and especially not by its clergy. Such dissensions among Carthaginian Christians could not but have weakened their communal response to persecution.

Conclusion

As discussed above, persecutions were represented to Christians as an effect of communal hostility. Now, thanks to Tertullian's testimony, we can see the various ways in which Christian organizations tried to foster a communal response to persecution. First, there is evidence that the clergy was successful in organizing a form of communal aid to Christians under arrest by providing them with food and moral support. Labeling defectors as heretics, or as "Gnostics" in the specific context of the second century, was probably also a efficacious means of reinforcing the boundaries of the community. Nevertheless, it is also clear that groupness did not arise throughout the whole membership and that the very diversity of responses to persecutions engendered tensions and dissensions that further weakened the communal response of Christians.

Tertullian also suggests that some Christians might temporarily set aside their membership, because they were prepared to deny being Christian before the authorities, or because they had decided to flee. However, as the question of flight from persecution suggests, we should be wary of accepting Tertullian's point of view on these matters. The defectors denounced as "Gnostics," for instance, might as well have opined that sacrifice or participation in civic festivals was not incompatible with their Christianness. The persecutions of the middle of the third century, to which we now turn, must be approached with similar caution, even if the circumstances are quite different.

Carthaginian Christians and the Edict of Decius (250)

It is a common assumption, based on a statement by Sulpicius Severus (*chron*. 2.32.1–3) and Cyprian's comment on the "long peace" that preceded the "persecution" of Decius (*laps*. 5), that between the end of the reign of Septimius Severus and the edict of Decius there were no persecutions. Timothy Barnes has forcefully denounced the fallaciousness of this reconstruction. In a letter dated to 251, Cyprian recalls the martyrdom of three forebears of the confessor Celerinus (*epist*. 39.3.1). The date of their martyrdom cannot be fixed with any certitude, but a plausible guess is c. 220 for Celerina and c. 240 for Laurentinus and Egnatius (Barnes 1971; 1985: 157–158; cf. Y. Duval 2001: 46–52; 2005: 242–244). In any case, it is clear that for Cyprian, preservation of the "peace," however long it truly was, was paramount (see below).

The events associated with the edict of Decius present a complex case study for examining the limits of religious allegiance among Christians. The correspondence of Cyprian, who was elected bishop of Carthage in 248, is an exceptional set of documents on the edict of Decius, its implementation in Carthage and the rest of North Africa, and its consequences for the Christian organization.[25] We must, first of all, form a clear understanding of the measure decided by Decius, and of how it affected the Christians. Then we will proceed to an examination of the various responses Christians in Carthage gave to the edict.

The Edict of Decius: Intent, Form, and Implementation

Decius was proclaimed emperor by his troops in May or June 249, and he subsequently marched on Rome and defeated the reigning emperor, Philip, in Verona in August or September of the same year. He then entered Rome and stayed there until summer 250 (Drinkwater 2005: 37–39). While in Rome he gave orders that all citizens sacrifice on behalf of the empire.[26] Few scholars still insist that the Christians were the target of Decius's edict, and there is no need to rehearse their arguments here.[27]

James Rives interestingly argues that the edict was "an important step towards a radical restructuring of religious organization in the Roman world" (1999: 135). It is unlikely, however, that the edict would have been perceived as such at the time; it is not even a well-established fact that Decius devised a new religious policy (see Selinger 2002: 27–32). Whether we view Decius's edict as an order to repeat the *supplicatio* traditionally associated with an emperor's accession (Selinger 2002: 44–45) or as the imposition of a specific script for the ceremony of the *nuncupatio votorum*, which was celebrated on January 3 on behalf of the emperor's personal welfare (Clarke 1984a: 25–26; 2005: 625), his measure was a unique and innovative event. Decius's intention was to restore the *pax deorum* in a very troubled period, and to this end he followed the model of Caracalla's citizenship law, orchestrating a sacrifice that was to be performed with universal participation (Brent 2010: 177–188).

The form and the implementation of Decius's edict are well known. That each required individual had in fact performed the sacrifice was to be certified by a board of local officials—there were five commissioners appointed in Carthage (Cyprian, *epist.* 43.3.1)—who would issue a signed and witnessed certificate (*libellus*). Enforcing such a measure does not seem to have been the administrative nightmare it might be imagined. Our knowledge of census and tax-collection procedures, particularly well documented in Egypt, shows that local magistrates knew how to oversee such proceedings (Rives 1999: 149–150). Altars for the event had been installed on the Capitol by the Forum (*laps.* 2, 8). A final date was set for all required people to have sacrificed (2, 3). Detected or reported recusants were heard by the local commission and, if they did not relent, deferred to the proconsul, who would conduct a second trial. Between the first and the second trial, the recalcitrant individuals were kept in prison. During the second trial, tortures could be applied to force compliance (see Clarke 1973a, 1973b). The penalty imposed seems to have been some variety of exile, sometimes accompanied by confiscation of property (*laps.* 2; Clarke 1984a: 35). When death occurred it was not by way of a legal sentence, but as a consequence of torture or imprisonment.

Hostility and Attacks against Christians

Though there is no evidence that Decius's edict targeted Christians, and even strong reasons to believe that this was not actually the case, the order to sacrifice seems to have generated some popular activity against Christians in Carthage.

Cyprian even attests to some hostility before the edict of Decius was known in Carthage. In Letter 7,[28] addressed to his clergy from an unknown location outside of Carthage, he explains why he is hiding, without making any allusion to the edict of Decius: "What I fear is that my presence may provoke an outburst of violence and resentment among the pagans and we thereby become responsible for the peace being broken" (*epist.* 7.1). He provides no details about what triggered this precise outburst before the edict was even known in Carthage. The hypothesis of a prior edict that had targeted only the clergy is now rejected (Clarke 1984a: 182–183, Deléani 2007: 126–127). The explanation could simply be Cyprian's nonparticipation in the celebrations accompanying the news of Decius's accession. In a letter written in 252 to the bishop of Rome, Cornelius, Cyprian reports that "in recent days, also, just as I am writing this letter to you, there has been once again popular outcry in the circus for him [Cyprian speaks of himself in the third person] to be thrown to the lion—this has been occasioned by the sacrifice which the people have been ordered to celebrate by a public edict" (*epist.* 59.6.1). Graeme W. Clarke has convincingly demonstrated that there was no persecution under the reign of Gallus (251–253), and he has suggested that the public edict here alluded to ordered the public performance of apotropaic sacrifices against the plague (1986: 4–17, 246–247). In both cases, it seems that Cyprian alone was the object of popular hostility. This was probably a consequence of his social standing and because, as a result of the development of the Christian organization, the bishop was now a public figure. It seems that hostility was not directed against the other Christians before the edict, but that some antagonism arose only after the edict was promulgated. However, Cyprian's references to popular hostility and attacks need to be analyzed carefully.

In one of the first letters written after the promulgation of the edict in Carthage, Cyprian mentions a presbyter and a layman "who sustained the people's first savage attack" (*epist.* 6.4). They are in prison at the time Cyprian writes the letter, which means that they have refused to comply when ordered to sacrifice. A similar case is attested in the town of Capsa, where some brothers, as it had been reported to Cyprian, "had withstood the violence of the magistrate and the attacks of the frenzied mob" (*epist.* 56.1.1). The mention of the magistrate suggests that the brothers were attacked after their refusal to sacrifice, once under arrest, and probably on their way to the prison (see Clarke 1984b: 197). In this case, it is legitimate to wonder whether Christians might have been the targets of popular hostility simply because they refused to sacrifice, and not primarily because they were Christians.

A very different incident is reported in Letter 40: "It was through his own words of encouragement that Numidicus sent on ahead of him a glorious band of martyrs, to be done to death by stones and flames, and it was with joy that he beheld the wife who clung to his side burnt to ashes (or, I should rather say, preserved) along with the others. Numidicus himself was half-burnt, buried under a pile of stones and left for dead" (*epist.* 40.1.1). Clarke comments: "This has all the air of a mob pogrom; it is no official execution when a prisoner can be left abandoned, undespatched" (1984b: 197). There is no doubt that these Christians were put to death outside any official procedure; whether the mob searched them out or came upon them at the end of one of their meetings, they were attacked before their refusal to sacrifice was confirmed in any official manner. However, we can only speculate, as the passage does not give any indication of the exact circumstances.

This is the extent of the evidence on popular hostility and attacks against Christians in Carthage. These incidents certainly might have contributed to a tense climate, but they cannot explain the way in which a substantial majority of Christians responded to the edict.

Christians' Answers to the Edict

Compliance

The majority response was to conform to the requirements of the imperial edict. Whether emphasizing the minority who resisted or the great number who did not, scholars are unanimous: the majority of Christians sacrificed.[29] This consensus is based on Cyprian's own testimony in several letters (*epist.* 11.1.2, 13.1, 14.1.1) and in the *De lapsis*, where he writes: "At the first threatening words of the Enemy, the greatest number (*maximus numerus*) of the brethren betrayed their faith" (*laps.* 7). Michael Sage suggests that "some exaggeration may be allowed" (1975: 192; cf. Clarke 1984a: 240 for rhetorical hyperbole), but it is not clear how it could have served Cyprian's purpose to exaggerate the number of the lapsed—either in a sermon in which he explains to them that they must perform an appropriate penance, or in letters to his clergy. If Cyprian exaggerates, it is in his description of Christians' eagerness to comply, as he clearly wants to emphasize the scandalousness of their attitude. Nevertheless, there is no ground for questioning the fact that the majority of Christians complied with the edict under no compulsion whatsoever.

In the eyes of Cyprian, these Christians "betrayed their faith" (*laps.* 7), and the only explanation he has to offer is their "attachment to their patrimony" (11).[30] Allen Brent rightly pointed out that fear for life and property does not fit well with the eagerness that Cyprian also attributes to them; fear could not have been the sole motive for the lapsed Christians (2010: 226). Instead, he suggests that Christians who participated in Decius's ceremony did so "because they sympathized with the aim of Decius' new proposal in terms of the construction of reality that they shared with their pagan contemporaries" (228). Where I depart from Brent's interpretation is the point at which he introduces the notion of "a popular syncretism" in which "Christian devotion" becomes one with "pagan impulse" (229–240). An analysis in terms of multiple memberships (or identities) is more economical. The idea that the lapsed did not activate their Christian membership in the context of their participation in this civic ceremony does away with the impossible task of defining what is "religious" for them. It also allows us to avoid the condescension implicit in Brent's estimation that the Christians cannot "trace logically the inconsistency" of their position (228). Cyprian does not invoke ignorance as a possible excuse.

If some Christians thought that they were betraying their Christian membership by participating in the sacrifice ordered by Decius—those who used the compromises that I describe next—this does not mean that all felt this way. Indeed, the majority of those who freely sacrificed expected to continue their membership. In the correspondence there is only one mention of lapsed "who after apostatizing, returned to the world which they had renounced and [now] live there as pagans" (*epist.* 57.3.1). In a few other cases, *sacrificati* are associated with heretics, but these texts make no allusion to actual people who have left the Christian organization (55.17.2, 59.11.3).

Compromises

Among the Christians who perceived a conflict between their membership and sacrificing, some pursued compromises. There were different means of obtaining a false certificate (*libellus*), and thus becoming a *libellaticus* (Brent 2010: 219–223). One option was to bribe a local official. Payments of bribes could be done in person or through a surrogate. Another option was to send a proxy to sacrifice on one's behalf.[31] In the eyes of Cyprian, all compromises are condemnable, and he does not elaborate greatly on the motivations of those who pursued them.

In Letter 55, however, Cyprian imagines the plea of a Christian who had obtained a false certificate: "I had previously read and I had learnt from my bishop's preaching that we should not offer sacrifice to idols and that a servant of God ought not to worship images. And so, in order to avoid doing this action which was forbidden, I seized an opportunity which offered itself for obtaining a certificate (which I would certainly not have acquired had there not presented itself such an opportunity). I either went up to the magistrate myself or I gave instructions to another who was on his way up to him.

I declared I was a Christian, that it was forbidden to me to offer sacrifice, that I could not approach the altars of the devil, and that I was, therefore, offering payment in order to avoid doing what was forbidden to me" (*epist.* 55.14.1). This imaginary plea, which is full of irony, suggests that Christians were approached by intermediaries who offered the possibility of obtaining a false certificate by bribing a magistrate. The Christians could thus excuse themselves as having merely taken an opportunity. They maintained that they knew Christians should not perform a sacrifice, and that they, accordingly, did not. In their case, fear is the most probable explanation for the compromise.

Flight

Another response was flight (Brent 2010: 240–247). As we have seen, Cyprian went into hiding before the edict of Decius was known in Carthage. Coming under strong criticism for his absence from Carthage at a time when some Christians were suffering hardship, he felt compelled to justify himself (Sage 1975: 192–196). In his letters, he explains why he remained away, but he does not concede that he fled persecution (Sage 1975: 193–194). In the *De lapsis*, nevertheless, without explicit reference to his own actions, Cyprian presents flight from persecution as an acceptable response: "If the primary claim to victory is that, having fallen into the hand of the pagans, a man should confess the Lord, the next title to glory is that he should have gone underground and preserved himself for further service of the Lord" (*laps.* 3). He also alludes to Jesus's command "If they persecute you in one city, flee to another" (Mt 10:23; *laps.* 10). There is no example of such flight in his correspondence: when we do hear of refugees, they are always Christians condemned to exile (*epist.* 21.4.1, 30.8.1, 55.13.2, 66.7.2).[32] Flight therefore was not a very common response among members of the Christian organization in Carthage.

Confession

Finally, some chose to refuse to sacrifice, and to confess to being Christian. The number of the confessors is difficult to evaluate—the number of martyrs was quite small, because death did not result from legal condemnation (see above). The group of confessors that Cyprian addresses in two of his letters does not seem to be very large (*epist.* 6, 10). In Letter 13 he mentions the amount of money he had sent for their support: to the 250 sesterces sent about two weeks ago he now adds another 250 sesterces of his own resources plus 175 sesterces given by the lector Victor (*epist.* 13.7). The sum of 250 sesterces was probably enough to support fifty persons for two weeks (Clarke 1984a: 259; Lo Cascio 2003: 300–302).

THE *STANTES*

There was also a group of Christians, sometimes called the *stantes*, who neither sacrificed nor confessed. They did not present themselves to the magistrates but somehow escaped their attention. For Cyprian, who groups them with those who fled, their glory is second only to that of the confessors: "Once the period prescribed for apostatizing had passed, whoever failed to declare himself within the time, thereby confessed that he was a Christian" (*laps.* 3). Geoffrey de Ste. Croix has called attention to this category, which had previously been somewhat overlooked (1954: 96). In the *De lapsis*, Cyprian says that their number was great (*multitudo stantium*; *laps.* 2), and in several letters he makes particular mention of the poor among them (*epist.* 12.2.2, 14.2.1).

Behind the variety of responses to Decius's edict, there were two basic positions: on the one hand, the majority of Christians did not consider the sacrifice relevant to their membership and accordingly performed it freely and willingly; on the other, a number of Christians did not want to sacrifice because of their membership. Some of the latter pursued compromises; others endured confession and martyrdom.

Christians were not targeted by the edict, and so there was little or no external pressure exerted on them as a group. There were only limited outbursts of popular hostility, and it is not clear that these were aimed at Christians per se rather than simply at individuals who did not sacrifice. Cyprian recommends that his clergy ensure that providing support to the confessors in prison does not engender hostility: the brethren have to avoid "visits in crowd and meeting in large numbers" (*epist.* 5.2.1); the clergy has to make sure that "the people who visit and meet together change and vary" (2.2). He wants to make sure that Christians do not by their attitude provoke hostility toward themselves as a group. Thus the Christians as a group did not seem to have been under attack, and Cyprian was concerned to see to it that this would remain true.

Is it Cyprian's desire "to ensure the general peace" (*epist.* 5.2.1) that explains why he at no point evokes or gives instructions to his clergy for preparing Christians to address the request of the edict? In the imaginary plea analyzed above, Cyprian clearly assumes that the instructions alluded to were received before the publication of the edict, as he mentions that they were issued by the bishop, who, as we know, was in hiding. Only those who refused to sacrifice and were arrested received encouragement in a letter that would fit the category of preparation for martyrdom (*epist.* 6; see Nicholson 2009 more generally on the topic).

As I have already pointed out, few Christians who performed the sacrifice anticipated renouncing their membership as a result. In fact, at least some clergy thought it unnecessary to impose any consequent conditions at all on the continuation of membership. Members of the Christian organization did not alter their behavior as Christians once they had sacrificed, but went to the regular gatherings and sought communion from the presbyters. At least some presbyters simply gave it to them. Such is the situation that we can reconstruct from Cyprian's correspondence. Already in Letter 14, the first written to his clergy after publication of the edict, Cyprian mentions a letter from some presbyters in which the issue seems to have been raised, and he intimates that the presbyters had already taken action either by granting an immediate reconciliation or by not requiring any reconciliation whatsoever (*epist.* 14.4, with Clarke 1984a: 268–269, Grattarola 1984: 4–5, and Deléani 2007: 284). In the final prayer of Letter 11, written shortly afterward, he asks that "repentance of the fallen may be restored" (*epist.* 11.8), a hint that some lapsed did not have to do penance. Controversy erupted once it became known in Carthage that the bishop had ordered his clergy to impose a penance on Christians who had sacrificed, and to suspend their reconciliation until a council had been convened to discuss the issue. It is impossible to establish an exact chronology of events, but it seems plausible that the lapsed began to ask confessors to provide them with certificates only after they were told that their reconciliation was not guaranteed. As attested by Cyprian himself, confessors and martyrs-to-be had, for the most part, no reservation about delivering such certificates, even collective ones (*epist.* 15.4).

There is no need to review in detail the controversy over the necessity of penance.[33] Before his return to Carthage, Cyprian conceded that the lapsed in danger of death should be reconciled immediately (*epist.* 18). The council of 251 confirmed his general policy of imposing penance on the *sacrificati* and reconciling them at death, but in 253 under Cyprian's guidance another council decided in favor of the collective reconciliation of all the lapsed. The reason invoked for this sudden change of policy was the renewal of threats against Christians, probably in the context of the plague rather than as a result of imperial policy, as there was no persecution under the reign of Gallus (see above). The *sacrificati* then reconciled had been in the ranks of the penitents for nearly three years and were asked to express thorough penance.

I have emphasized that the category "Christian" was not relevant to Decius's decision to publish his edict or to its implementation. I have also suggested that the ensuing episodes of popular hostility were aimed at those who did not sacrifice rather than at Christians per se. Finally, Cyprian himself, by going into hiding, and issuing instructions to his clergy, ensured that Christians did not become a target. In the end, the fact that the category "Christian" did not matter much in this context, neither to the majority of the members of the Christian organization nor to the non-Christians, is consistent with a rather low level of Christian groupness throughout these events.

Valerian's Persecution (257–260)

The next episode of persecution documented in North Africa began in the summer of 257 with the arrival of a letter from the emperors Valerian and Gallienus asking the governor to search out bishops and presbyters so that they might "acknowledge the Roman rites" (*Pass. Cypr.* 1.1).[34] This is the context of Cyprian's convocation before the proconsul Aspasius Paternus and, after his refusal to comply, of his relegation to the city of Curubis (Sage 1975: 337–347). Though the proconsul mentions that he is also supposed to search for presbyters, there is no indication that he did so after Cyprian had refused to give him their names. Last, the proconsul also announces that the emperors forbade the Christians to hold assemblies and to enter the *coemeteria*.

Through the correspondence of Cyprian we know that the orders of Valerian and Gallienus were also implemented in Numidia. There, not only nine bishops but also presbyters, deacons, and even some laypeople had been condemned to the mines (*epist.* 76–79). The disparate treatments of Cyprian and the Numidians can be explained by their difference in status: as an *honestior*, Cyprian could not be sent to the mines (Clarke 1989: 278). The presence of lay men, women, and children among the Numidians is more difficult to explain: it is quite likely that they disobeyed the interdiction against holding assemblies (285).

A year later, the emperors sent new instructions to the governors: bishops, presbyters, and deacons were to be put to death immediately; senators, high-ranking officials, and equestrians were to lose their status and their property and were to suffer capital punishment if they persisted in their faith; matrons were to be dispossessed and sent into exile; freedmen of the imperial household were to lose their freedom (*epist.* 80.1.2, with Clarke 1989: 300–305). This is the background to the execution of Cyprian on September 14, 258.

In addition to the letters of Cyprian, two *Passions* document persecutions in North Africa: the *Passion of Marian and James* and the *Passion of Lucius and Montanus*. Though both texts betray the strong literary influence of the *Passion of Perpetua and Felicitas*, they are thought to contain reliable information on the circumstances of the martyrdoms (Lanata 1973: 86; see Lomanto 1975). The circumstances described in the *Passion of Marian and James* match what we know about Valerian's persecution. Marian, who is a lector, James, who is a deacon, and the narrator, who seems to be a layman, were en route to Numidia. They happened to stay at a house where also lodged two bishops recalled from exile in order to be tried in conformity with the second edict of Valerian (*Pass. Mar. Iac.* 2–3). Two days later, soldiers came to the place and arrested all present (4). Marian's and James's membership in the clergy is explicitly established (5). The *Passion* also mentions an equestrian (8).

A Christian Riot?

The circumstances of the arrest of the martyrs in the *Passion of Lucius and Montanus* are less clear and have been the object of a recent hypothesis that needs to be discussed.[35]

The eight martyrs named at the beginning of the *Passion* are usually presented as victims of the second set of instructions of Valerian and Gallienus. The text does not explicitly confirm this, but the circumstances of their arrest are described in the following terms: "We were arrested after a popular riot which a wild crowd had aroused for the purpose of killing the governor, and after violence had been engineered to produce a fierce pogrom of Christians on the following day" (*Pass. Montan.* 2.1). Pio Franchi de' Cavalieri, who first pointed out this interesting reading in one of the best manuscripts, interprets the facts as follows: there was a popular riot in which the life of the governor was threatened, and this was subsequently blamed on the Christians (1909: 15).

Timothy Barnes, who recently called scholars' attention to this reading, now confirmed by François Dolbeau's critical edition (1983), suggests that the riot might have been instigated by the Christians (Barnes 2009: 9–14, repeated in Barnes 2010: 86–92). His arguments are as follows: (1) the *Passion of Lucius and Montanus* reports that soldiers told the martyrs "that the governor was 'uttering threats in a rage over the events of the previous day' and proposing to burn them alive" (2010: 90–91, quoting *Pass. Montan.* 3.1); (2) this governor is Galerius Maximus, the proconsul of 258–259, who was extremely ill at the time of Cyprian's arrest and who died a few days after his execution (2010: 91–92, quoting *Pass. Cypr.* 2 and 5); (3) when Pontius, on the first anniversary of Cyprian's martyrdom, writes the *Life of Cyprian*, he does not mention the illness or the death of Galerius Maximus, thus betraying the embarrassment of the Christians regarding these events (2010: 92).

Barnes does not elaborate on how we should interpret this Christian riot, which would have followed the execution of Cyprian, beyond describing it as "unexpected evidence of the political power of the Christian community in Carthage" (2009: 9).[36] However, if we accept Barnes's hypothesis, we have here a situation in which some Christians—not all of them, but a significant number—acted as a group whose principle of coherence was their membership in the Christian organization. Unfortunately Barnes's case is not entirely convincing.[37]

First, Barnes leaves unexamined the serious chronological problems with the identification of the governor targeted by the crowd as Galerius Maximus (on these problems, see Franchi de' Cavalieri 1909: 13–16). Second, the mention of the procurator acting governor in place of the dead proconsul at the time of the first hearing of the martyrs—if not merely a reminiscence of the *Passion of Perpetua and Felicitas*—does not necessarily imply that the proconsul who died is the one targeted by the riot. The *Passion* uses the term *praeses* in a fairly loose way throughout the narrative, and the succession of the magistrates involved cannot be definitively reconstructed. Finally, Pontius, contrary to Barnes's claims, mentions the illness of Galerius Maximus in a manner consistent with the narrative of the *Acts* (Pontius, *V. Cypr.* 15.8, with Bastiaensen 1975: 272). If Galerius Maximus, responsible for the execution of Cyprian, is eliminated as the possible target of the riot, what could have been the Christians' motive for instigating a riot? It seems more probable to understand that, whatever its cause, the violence of the mob was blamed on the Christians and that in reprisal Christians were harassed in a particularly severe way. In the end, the *Passion of Marian and James* is just another example of a Christian text presenting Christians as the target of some form of communal hatred.

However, in the *Acts of Cyprian*, there is mention of a Christian collective reaction after Cyprian's death sentence was pronounced by Galerius Maximus: "After the sentence, the crowd of brothers said: 'Let us also be beheaded with him'. The result of this was an uproar of the brothers, and a great throng followed him" (*Pass. Cypr.* 4.1). It does not say much about the "political power" of the Christians in Carthage, but it suggests that at least in this particular circumstance Christians saw themselves and their bishop as one body.

Epilogue: The "Great Persecution"

Immediately after the capture of Valerian by the Persian king Shapur in the summer of 260, his son Gallienus not only canceled the edict of persecution but ordered the restitution of all confiscated properties to the bishops (Eusebius Caesariensis, *HE* 7.13; Clarke 2005: 645–646). As Barnes has recently reaffirmed (2010: 97–99), the importance of this edict for the Christians and their status in the Roman Empire has too often be neglected in favor of the so-called edict of Milan. Indeed, it amounted to a full legalization of Christianity, and no Christian seems to have been executed on account of his religious beliefs between 260 and 303. Barnes has rightly emphasized that the cases of the "military martyrs" are only apparent exceptions, insofar as the documentation shows that it is the martyrs themselves who thought that their religion was not compatible with military service.[38]

The Nature of the Persecution in North Africa

On February 23, 303, imperial persecution resumed with an edict of Diocletian that ordered the destruction of churches and the burning of all copies of the scriptures and forbade the holding of Christian assemblies. It also targeted some categories of Christians: those with legal privileges lost them, and imperial freedmen were reduced to slavery. Finally, it required the performance of a sacrifice before any official business be conducted (Eusebius Caesariensis, *HE* 8.2.4; Eusebius, *Mart. Pal.* praef. 1; Lactantius, *Mort. Pers.* 12–13; see De Ste. Croix 1954: 75–76). This, the first of the four edicts of Diocletian,[39] was the only one that was promulgated in North Africa. There, the fourth edict of February 304, in particular, which imposed a sacrifice on all inhabitants of the Empire, was not enforced (De Ste. Croix 1954: 88–92). We do not hear about *lapsi* in Africa as we do in Egypt or in Asia Minor, with the exception of a few bishops who might have been asked to sacrifice at the same time as they surrendered the scriptures (the accusation is indeed rare during the Donatist controversy: De Ste. Croix 1954: 89). The persecution must have stopped soon after May 305, when Constantius became Augustus of the West, even if the official cancellation of the edict of Diocletian did not happen before the winter of 306–307, when Maxentius took control of Italy and Africa (Barnes 2010: 150).[40]

As De Ste. Croix rightly pointed out, the first edict of Diocletian outlawed only the "collective practice" of Christianity: "merely 'being a Christian' (the *nomen Christianum*) was visited with only one penalty: deprivation of the use of legal process" (1954: 77). Thus, the nature of the "Great Persecution" as enforced in Africa explains why, despite abundant documentation and a long list of martyrs, there is so little material illustrating the responses of individuals, particularly of laypersons.

Enforcement of the Edict of 303

The mechanism of enforcement of the edict of 303 in Africa is particularly well-documented and has been commented on many times (see Barnes 2010:

128–138 for a brief review). The *Acts of Felix of Thibiuca* recounts the case of a bishop who refused to give up the scriptures (Lepelley 1979–81: vol. 1, 335; vol. 2, 192–193), while the *Acts of Gallonius* and the *Acts of the Martyrs of Abithina* tell of Christians who held assemblies despite the imperial interdiction (Lancel 1999 and Lepelley 1999 on the *Acts of Gallonius*; Lepelley 1979–81: vol. 1, 335–336 and vol. 2, 58–60 on the *Acts of the Martyrs of Abithina*). However, as Claude Lepelley has suggested (1979–81: vol. 1, 337–343), several documents show that pagans and Christians seemed to have reached an understanding: the municipal authorities would comply *a minimo* with the requirements of the imperial edicts, and the Christians would keep quiet until better times.

This is well illustrated by the case of Abthugni, a small city fifty miles southwest of Carthage, known thanks to its bishop's later involvement in the Donatist controversy; Felix was among the bishops who elected Caecilianus to the see of Carthage.[41] When Felix was tried in 314 or 315 for having surrendered the scriptures, Alfius Caecilianus, the local magistrate in charge of the implementation of the edict of 303, testified as to his own conduct at that time. It appears that Felix was in fact absent from Abthugni when the magistrate came to seize the scriptures, hence his exculpation. The local officials were content with the destruction of the throne (*cathedra*) and with the burning of a few documents that were found,[42] and no further persecutory measures were taken against any of the Christians in the city. The bishop seems to have been on friendly terms with the magistrate (Frend 1985: 4; Lepelley 1979–81: vol. 1, 339–340), and indeed the Christians themselves, as it is reported, sent representatives to ask him what measures he intended to take to implement the emperor's edict (Optatus, *app.* 2.4). Alfius Caecilianus is an example of a local magistrate who was eager to implement the imperial edict, but who was inspired by no religious zeal whatsoever; he seems to have viewed the religious allegiance of the Christians as merely an administrative category. From examples like this, scholars have deduced the peaceful coexistence of the Christians and pagans. In my view, these cases actually illustrate that religious allegiance played a rather circumscribed role in the everyday life of the inhabitants of Abthugni, whether Christian or not, with the result that they could share the city as a "neutral ground" (see Lepelley 2002).

Conclusion

Persecution was not a constant threat in the everyday life of Christians, even before the "Minor Peace of the Church," as the period inaugurated by the edict of Gallienus in 260 is sometimes called in anticipation of the "Peace of

Church" ushered in by Constantine.[43] Popular hatred appears to have been, at least in part, a construct of the Christians who were trying to mobilize their brothers rather than a social reality accompanied by all manner of abuses. The picture that has emerged in this chapter is thus rather consistent with the conclusions of chapter 1: not only did Christians share a number of memberships with non-Christians, but Christians and non-Christians alike did not necessarily or consistently regard their religious allegiance as more significant than other memberships. Thus, when Decius ordered all inhabitants of the Roman Empire to sacrifice to the gods for the restoration of order and security, the majority of Christians complied, as it was a requirement of their membership in the imperial commonwealth. They did this either unaware that it might be contradictory to their Christian membership, or because they simply did not activate their Christian membership in this context, at least not until they were challenged to do so by Cyprian and his clergy.

Despite Tertullian's rhetorical threats in the *Ad Scapulam* and Barnes's fragile hypothesis about a Christian riot in 259, there is very little evidence that Christians addressed the authorities as a group in the context of the persecution. Throughout the enforcement of Decius's edict, Cyprian did all he could to avoid Christians being targeted as a group, while making it clear that the sacrifice was not compatible with Christian faith. As Lucy Grig (2004) has shown, "making martyrs" was more of a project in the fourth century than in the second and the third.

Now that we have completed our picture of everyday Christianity in the pre-Constantinian period, we will proceed to a comparable analysis of the Theodosian period. Before proceeding, however, I want to note again the century-long gap in our sources (see above in the introduction). Aside from those documents related to the "Great Persecution" and to the Donatist schism, there is very little evidence on fourth-century North Africa. The two African apologists, Arnobius and Lactantius, both died before the end of Constantine's reign, and their writings, circumscribed by the traditions of the apologetic mode, are of little use to the student of everyday social experience. This paucity of evidence precludes a detailed understanding of the "Constantinian revolution," but some light can be shed on these years through a comparison of the pre-Constantinian and the Theodosian periods.

CHAPTER 3

Being Christian in the Age of Augustine

Our study resumes with Augustine's ordination as bishop of Hippo in 395 (for the date, see Lancel 2002: 184–185). The status of Christians in the Roman Empire has changed greatly in the interim. By this time Christianity has been legal in North Africa for nearly a hundred years, a fact that, as Augustine reminds his audience (*serm.* 62.15), makes a crucial difference to Christians' standing in the Empire. In several texts, he derides the pagans as now being only a tiny minority that lives in fear and shame (*serm.* 198auct [Dolbeau 26].8; *serm.* 306B [Denis 18].6; *cons. euang.* 1.14.21; see Madec 1992: 28–29). In a sermon preached in Bulla Regia, he goes so far as to assume that there are no longer any pagans in the city (*serm.* 301A [Denis 17].7). These statements cannot be taken as evidence on the actual number of pagans, but they do suggest that "Christian" is not, by this period, a marked category, that of the "special" or the "other," but an unmarked category, that of the taken-for-granted, while "pagan" has now become a marked category (on marked and unmarked categories, see Brubaker et al. 2006: 211–212). We will see that this is, in fact, an accurate assessment in some senses, but erroneous in others.

The Theodosian age is traditionally presented as the period of the triumph of Christianity and the death of paganism. However, as Peter Brown warns us, we need to be mindful of the fact that this "representation" was the construct of "a brilliant generation of Christian writers" (Brown 1998: 633; see also 1995). Likewise, the series of laws (or rather their extracts preserved in the *Theodosian Code*) that outlaw paganism and pagans and order the closing of temples and the destruction of statues have also been interpreted by modern scholars as the result of a general religious policy, but most of these laws are in fact reactive and address local situations (Errington 1997, 2006). As a preliminary observation, we should note that the closure of temples and the ban on all ritual practices associated with traditional Greco-Roman cults did not amount to a Christianization of public life. As Claude Lepelley has demonstrated most clearly, not only did the clergy have no hold over municipal institutions, but these institutions remained unchanged (Lepelley 1979–81: vol. 1, 371–376). Augustine did not live in a Christian world, but in a world in which Christians and non-Christians shared the city—both its space and, for the most part, its values. The multifaceted aspects of the "secular" in late antiquity have been thoroughly examined in recent years (see Rebillard and Sotinel 2010). This "secular" should not be seen as a mere byproduct of Christianization, since religious pluralism had been a de facto situation for years before Christianity was a legal religious option (North 1992).

The idea that the fourth and fifth centuries saw the development of a secular realm before its contraction in the sixth century is one of the major contributions of Robert Markus (1970, 1990) to the understanding of the period. However, the division of everyday life between sacred and secular, or between religious and nonreligious, presupposes a model of behavior that is both too rigid and too dependent on a Christian theological point of view.[1] The situational approach that I sketched in the introduction is a model that seems to account for the evidence more satisfactorily: it better accommodates both individual variations and variations within each individual's behavior.

Augustine's Letters and Sermons: The Evidence and Its Limitations

The core of the evidence used in this chapter is selected letters and sermons of Augustine.[2] The dialogic nature of letter writing is self-evident, and ancient theorists of epistolography have consistently presented the letter exchange as a dialogue. Drawing from literary approaches to letter writing (Rousset 1962; Altman 1982), Jen Ebbeler has recently emphasized that, since dialogue is constitutive to it, the letter exchange is a "performative space," and that we need to pay attention to "strategies for managing epistolary relationships," as the letter exchange can be "manipulated to script a textual identity for oneself and for one's correspondent" (Ebbeler 2001: 163, 167–168). Analysis of a few letter exchanges preserved in Augustine's correspondence, in particular with laypeople, thus provides interesting documentation of conflicting scripts about being Christian.

Augustine's sermons were, for the most part, delivered extemporaneously, and numerous features, such as their conversational tone and irregularities of syntax, evidence their spontaneity. They were recorded by stenographers, who took notes in shorthand during the delivery and then transcribed them in longhand (Deferrari 1922; Olivar 1991: 911–914). Augustine kept copies of his sermons in his library in Hippo, as is attested by the Possidian catalog (Dolbeau 1998). Not all the extant sermons transmitted under Augustine's name were preserved in their original state, but as a result, in particular, of the recent discoveries of François Dolbeau, we are now in a better position to determine whether a sermon is complete or not (Dolbeau 1993: 421–423). What was invariably cut by copyists were allusions to the actual delivery. However, a good number of sermons still evince the actual process of communication between the preacher and his audience, and such a process implies a dialogism of the sort that is at work in the letter exchange. Just as the letter writer manipulates his addressee, so the preacher manipulates his audience by presenting it with a script that can be deconstructed only through careful reading. The sermons also reflect how an actual exchange with the audience could, over time, lead Augustine to partly incorporate his audiences' points of view (Rebillard 1997; Uhalde 2007). The sermons can therefore provide good evidence for when and how Christianity mattered in everyday life.

By limiting my investigation to Augustine and his audience, I also limit it to only one of the several competing organizations claiming the name of "Christian" in fourth- and fifth-century North Africa. The long-standing division between the Catholics and the Donatists is well known (Frend 1985), but direct evidence on the Donatists is so scarce that they cannot be usefully included in this study. Although their ecclesiology can be successfully reconstructed beyond the stereotype of the "Church of the Pure" (Tilley 1997), it is impossible to get a sense of the representations that laypeople had of their identity as Christians. The Donatist sermons recently discovered (Leroy 1999; Schindler 2003) are too decontextualized to allow the kind of analysis that I conduct here.[3]

According to Augustine, the Manichaeans also considered themselves Christians: they were the "true Christians" (*util. cred.* 14.36), while the Catholics were "half-Christians" (*c. Faust.* 1.3). Despite recent attempts (in particular BeDuhn 2000) to reconstruct the practices that identified the Manichaeans, for the historian Manichaeanism remains mainly a body of doctrines, and our sources provide no evidence about the individuals who recognized themselves as members of this sect.[4] For this reason, these Christians also are excluded from the present study.

The other limit of my investigation pertains to the social range of the persons addressed by Augustine in his sermons. We should not adopt Ramsay MacMullen's (1989) pessimistic view, according to which Augustine and the other major preachers of the fourth and fifth centuries whose sermons are extant had "a distinctly upper-class audience" (for an "optimistic view," see Rousseau 1998). Nevertheless, Augustine's audience was not representative of all the persons who would have been identified as Christian in the diocese of Hippo or in the city of Carthage. Leslie Dossey, for instance, compares the sermons preached to the *competentes*, those members of Augustine's regular audience whom he was preparing for baptism, and the sermons preached to the newly baptized, when his audience comprised Christians from the entire diocese of Hippo, including, for example, the rustic decurion Curma (*cur. mort.* 12.15; Harmless 1995: 244–245). Dossey shows that "for most of the year Augustine's audience was composed of property-owning *urbani*, with a mixture of more humble outsiders on special occasions" (2010: 149–153, quote at 150). We need to be aware of this limitation, but we must also acknowledge that these are the only Christians whose self-understanding remains accessible to modern scholars.

Defining Christian Membership

Who was regarded as Christian in the "Catholic Church" as defined by Augustine? The nature of the available evidence does not allow us to consider self-ascription. There is of course the famous example of Marius Victorinus, the Roman professor of rhetoric, in Augustine's *Confessions*. Simplicianus, presbyter of the Church of Milan, when he tells the story to Augustine, reports that one day toward the end of his life Victorinus told him that he had become a Christian, and that he replied that he would count him among the faithful the day he would see him in church (*conf.* 8.2.4). The anecdote needs to be read in the context of Augustine's own conversion narrative, and, as the case of Victorinus is clearly exceptional, it has rather limited value as evidence on self-ascription.

Christian status was technically acquired with the *signatio*, that is, when the sign of Christ, the cross, was received on the forehead. With this and a few other rites, such as the sacrament of salt and exorcism rites, the candidate was admitted to the catechumenate (Van der Meer 1961: 354–356; Lamirande 1992: 792–793; Harmless 1995: 150–151). As attested in the *De catechizandis rudibus*, these rites were preceded by a single instructional session, which could be as short as half an hour.

Catechumens were Christian, but not yet faithful: "Ask a man if he is a Christian. If he is a pagan or a Jew he will immediately answer 'No', but if he says 'Yes', then ask him further whether he is a catechumen or one of the faithful" (*in euang. Ioh.* 44.2). What, then, was the difference between the catechumens and the faithful? The faithful had been baptized, and with baptism came salvation. An allocution among the Dolbeau sermons makes clear what is at stake in the distinction: The bishop of a town through which Augustine was traveling invited him to make use of his authority and to explain to a rich family why their son, who had died unbaptized, could not be buried in a church. Augustine takes this opportunity to remind his audience that eternal death is the fate of the unbaptized, and he urges all catechumens to seek baptism (*serm.* 142auct. [Dolbeau 7], with Harmless 2004: 20–23).

Similar calls to baptism are frequent in Augustine's preaching, and scholars in the past have been inclined to see in the catechumenate "the customary status of the nominal Christian, the man who lacked the courage for baptism but was ashamed to be called a heathen" (Van der Meer 1961: 357; see Saxer 1988: 424). However, most of these calls were preached at the approach of Lent, the period of the year during which catechumens were invited to register for baptism at Easter. There is, consequently, insufficient evidence to support the claim that postponement of baptism was a widespread practice, and the stereotype of masses of indifferent catechumens who delay baptism until death should be abandoned definitively (Rebillard 1998: 288–289, with Harmless 2004: 23–24).

There was no ecclesiastical rule about the proper age for baptism. It seems to have been common practice that infants were made catechumens, as was the case with Augustine himself (*conf.* 1.11.17; 6.4.5), but that baptism was received in adulthood. Suzanne Poque (1987) has shown that, although infant baptism was a topic of theological debate, Augustine himself considered adult baptism to be normal practice. From his sermons it appears that infants were baptized only in case of emergency, such as a life-threatening illness. In one text Augustine evokes the heavy responsibilities attached to raising baptized children (*in psalm.* 50.24), but in none of the preserved sermons does he invite parents to baptize infants. In the *De catechizandis rudibus*, where only adults are considered, no recommendation is given about how long one should remain a catechumen before seeking baptism. If there was a social consensus about the appropriate age for baptism, it escapes the historian.

The distinction between the catechumens and the faithful was, nevertheless, relevant to the self-understanding of Christians and to their identification by others. Catechumens benefited from a form of leniency. In a sermon in which he complains about the crowd celebrating the *natalis civitatis* of

Carthage, Augustine thus says: "I take it, beloved, that you have assembled today in greater numbers than usual in order to pray for those who are kept away by their perverted and unworthy mania. We are not speaking of pagans, or of Jews, but of Christians; and not even of our catechumens, but of many baptized persons" (*in psalm.* 50.1). In his *Commentary on Galatians*, he ironically recalls that the faithful regularly consult astrologers but that they cannot tolerate that even catechumens participate in the Jewish Sabbath (*in Gal.* 35). These incidental comments attest that this leniency was the norm, as Augustine suggests in the *Confessions*: "Why is it that we still hear nowadays people saying on all sides of many another person, 'Let him be, let him do as he likes; he is not baptized yet'?" (*conf.* 1.11.18).

In several sermons Augustine suggests that some catechumens might have used their status as an argument for demanding lower expectations. In a sermon in which he comments on the call of Mark 1:15 ("Repent and believe in the gospel"), Augustine explains that "Believe in the gospel" is addressed to the pagans, while "Repent" is addressed to all Christians, including not only those who take their religion seriously, but also catechumens and careless faithful. He then specifically refutes the possible objection of a catechumen: "A catechumen can answer me, 'Why say Repent to us? First let me become one of the faithful, and perhaps I shall live a good life, and I won't have to be a penitent'" (*serm.* 352A [Dolbeau 14].3). In another sermon, he condemns theatergoing: "And this is done by Christians; I'd rather not say, and by the faithful. A catechumen, perhaps, has a low opinion of his worth. 'I'm just a catechumen,' he says. You're a catechumen? 'Yes, a catechumen.' Do you have one forehead on which you received the sign of Christ, and another which you carry along to the theater? Do you want to go? Change your forehead, and get along there. So, as you can't change your forehead, don't ruin it" (*serm.* 301A [Denis 17].8). In both cases, however, Augustine's answers to the objections illustrate the inclusiveness of his pastoral preaching: all Christians, both catechumens and the faithful, are addressed. In fact, as has been rightly emphasized (Harmless 1995: 156–158; also 2004: 24–25), catechumens did not receive special instruction. Only rarely did Augustine speak to them directly and usually very briefly: twenty-two times among more than five hundred sermons preserved (Harmless 1995: 191–192 for a chart). Consequently, I will not, for the most part, attempt to distinguish between catechumens and the faithful in the remainder of this chapter.

Neither the instructions to the catechumens nor those to the newly baptized contain explicit rules about membership maintenance. For instance, the ecclesiastical legislation as we know it through the canons of the African councils does not prescribe any rule relative to Mass attendance. Unless one apostatized, Christian membership could not be lost. The *excommunicati*, faithful who had been given a public penance, were Christian: they had their place in the church, even if they were cut off from the rest of the congregation (Van der Meer 1961: 151–152).

Expressing Christian Membership

We need now to consider how Christians identified themselves to others—in other words, we will ask by what social mechanisms they expressed their Christianness. This will enable us to begin assessing the circumstances in which Christianness was activated.

External Markers

We can quickly eliminate looks, clothing, speech, and even occupations as markers of Christian membership in fourth-century North Africa. Christians did not dress in any specific way; even the clergy do not seem to have worn any special distinguishing dress. When Possidius describes Augustine's style of clothing, he says only that it was "simple and adequate, neither ostentatious, nor particularly poor" (Possidius, *vita Aug.* 22). When one wished to become Christian, the interrogation of inquirers, as described in the *De catechizandis rudibus*, focused on motives, not on lifestyle or profession. Even an astrologer could continue to practice his trade, as is attested by the case discussed by Augustine in a sermon he preached in Carthage (*in psalm.* 61.23).

Nor is there much to be said regarding Christian onomastics. The names of Christians were only rarely a marker of their religious identity. Despite debates over what makes a name "Christian" (Choat 2006: 51–56), all scholars agree that Christian names were not common in late antiquity (Kajanto 1963; Marrou 1977; Pietri 1977). In North Africa, 15 to 20 percent is a generous estimate for specifically Christian names among the Christians of Carthage, Mactar, and Haïdra (N. Duval 1977: 453). Changing a name at baptism, while not an unknown practice, occurred only rarely in late antiquity (Kajanto 1963: 118–121; Horsley 1987: 6–8). Although John Chrysostom does recommend in one sermon that Christian parents give names of saints to their children (*In Gen.* 21.3; Kajanto 1963: 92), Augustine offers no such advice in his extant corpus.

Churchgoing

The most obvious way to make one's Christianity public was through churchgoing or attendance at Mass. This would have been true even though churches were probably not closed to non-Christians, and we have evidence for the presence of pagans in Augustine's audience. One of the sermons discovered by François Dolbeau is preserved along with valuable indications on the circumstances under which it was given: Augustine was visiting the small town of Boseth in 404, and pagans came to hear him preach. The stenographer also noted when they left the church at the end of the sermon. After their departure, Augustine briefly urged his audience, now composed only of Christians, to encourage conversions by making their own lives exemplary (*serm.* 360A [Dolbeau 25].28) Notwithstanding, churchgoing would be, in most cases, a clear marker of Christian identity.

As far as we know, there were no rules about churchgoing or about the frequency of communion for the baptized. In any event, Augustine did not think it important to spell out any such rules in his sermons. Mass was celebrated daily in the morning, and Christians might also gather for vespers (Van der Meer 1961: 172). However, several allusions in the sermons make it clear that the Christians who were attending these weekday gatherings, morning and evening, singled themselves out in the eyes of other Christians (*serm.* 306B [Denis 18].6; *in psalm.* 49.23, 66.3). When Augustine says that people who go to church on Saturdays are particularly "hungry for the word of God" (*serm.* 128.6), it is difficult to decide if he is merely being wry because his audience is becoming restless or if he is suggesting that only strongly motivated Christians attend Mass on that day.

On a number of occasions Augustine notes that his church is unusually crowded on important feast days (Van der Meer 1961: 169–170), which suggests that not all Christians regularly attended Mass on Sundays or even on minor feast days. Therefore, we need to keep in mind that the Christians whose everyday Christianity we discuss in this chapter are not necessarily representative of average Christians. By this I do not refer to their social status (see above), but to their self-identification as Christians through attending Mass.

Church and Life-Cycle Rituals

Another possible indicator of Christian identity was the presence of the bishop and/or other members of the clergy at events marking important points in the life cycle. We need to keep in mind that, in this period, the bishops neither imposed nor even proposed specific Christian rituals for birth and name giving, marriage, or death and burial.

The traditional Roman ceremony of name giving on the eighth day after birth is well documented (Tels-de Jong 1959: 111–129). Tertullian had thought it proper for a Christian to accept an invitation to such a ceremony at the house of a relative or a neighbor (*idol.* 16.1), and there are some later mentions of the ceremony (Arnobius, *nat.* 3.4; Ausonius, *parent.* 11.8; Macrobius, *sat.* 1.16.36), but none in Augustine. In any case, as we have already noted, Christians typically did not give their children a name that was specifically Christian. There is no description of the entrance of infants into the catechumenate, so we do not know whether this event was marked by some celebration at church or at home. Baptism of infants was not common, as we have seen, and its performance in case of impending death was probably very informal.

We do know more about marriage. David Hunter (2003) has clearly demonstrated that, in North Africa, none of the Christianized rituals of marriage that were common in Italy had become established before or during Augustine's lifetime. Consequently, nothing would have distinguished a pagan wedding from a Christian one, unless the bishop had been invited into the family home and asked to sign the marriage contract. Augustine refers several times to these contracts, the *tabulae matrimoniales*, and attests to the practice of the bishop signing them along with other witnesses (*serm.* 332.4; *in psalm.* 149.15; Possidius, *vita Aug.* 27.5; see Hunter 2003: 75–76). There is no reason to assume that all Christians invited a bishop to their marriage ceremony, but this practice was clearly an expression of Christianness.

Bishops and clergy were not involved in a Christian's funeral and burial except by the family's request (Rebillard 2009b: 123–139). Thus the Council of Hippo in 393 reveals that some families brought their deceased to church and asked for a Eucharistic service to be celebrated (*Concilium Hipponense a.* 393, c. 4). At the request of the family, the clergy might have participated in the funeral procession, but there is no positive evidence for this in North Africa.[5] Most Christians were buried in a space that not only escaped the control of the clergy but was not necessarily marked as Christian. However, the choice of a burial place could also have been a marker of Christian identity, as in the case of the family who wanted their unbaptized son to be buried in a church (Aug. *serm.* 142auct. [Dolbeau 7]; see Yasin 2009 on burial churches in North Africa).[6] It was also possible to mark one's last resting place as that of a Christian by the use of unambiguous Christian symbols and/or formulas on the tomb or in the epitaph (N. Duval 1988; Pietri 1997: vol. 3, 1407–1468; Carletti 2008: 68–74).

This review of possible expressions of Christian identity does not claim to be exhaustive. Two main types of markers have been observed: participation in communal activities and the association of the clergy with life-cycle rituals that are part of the private sphere. It is more difficult to draw conclusions about the inclusion of fellow Christians who would not normally be part of these events. One thinks, for instance, of Augustine's recommendation that the poor be invited to banquets commemorating the family dead (*epist.* 22.6; Quasten 1940). However, we know of no specific examples of such inclusion and cannot say how common it might have been.

I have suggested several times that most of these markers were optional, and not obligations imposed by ecclesiastical authority. It is important to realize that not all Christians chose to identify themselves as such in all these ways. We now need to consider behaviors that reflect more internalized beliefs about what it meant to be Christian.

The Logic of the Actors

Historians have been forcefully reminded that not everybody went through a conversion process of the sort described by Augustine in the *Confessions* (MacMullen 1984, criticizing Nock 1933). Considerable energy also has been devoted to exploring "how much of their past the converts of the fourth century carried into church with them" (MacMullen 1984: 85; cf. 1997, 2009). However, most scholars have simply adopted the criteria of the bishops to determine what was "religious," and given too little consideration to the arguments used by Christians when they were challenged by their bishops to justify their behavior. These exchanges reflect something of the logic of the actors and thus supply important evidence on Christians' self-understanding.

Scriptural Legalism

We have already encountered in Tertullian one of the recurrent means of justification: scriptural legalism, or the attempt to use a text from the scriptures as evidence that a behavior under scrutiny is either justified or forbidden.

Discussions about funerary meals (for background, see Rebillard 2005) suffice to illustrate how scriptural justification was used.[7] In Letter 22 to Aurelius, the bishop of Carthage, whom he tries to enroll in his fight against the practice, Augustine quotes Romans 13:13–14: "Not in feasting and drunkenness, not in fornication and impurity, not in strife and jealousy; rather, put on the Lord Jesus Christ, and do not provide for the flesh with its desires." Just as fornication and impurity are banned from the church, explains Augustine, so should feasting and drunkenness be banned; thus meals should be banned from the tombs of the saints and the churches (*epist.* 22.1.3). Later in the same letter, on the topic of private funerary meals, he adds: "It seems to me to be easier to dissuade them from this foul and shameful practice if it is also forbidden by the scriptures" (1.6). Augustine here legitimizes the Christians' demand that bishops ground their rulings in scripture.

However, Christians also tried to use scriptural passages to contest the authority of their bishop. In Sermon 361, Augustine makes the general claim that scripture does not refer to the commemorative ceremony for the dead known as the *parentalia*: "And it's obvious that this doesn't benefit the dead, and that it's a custom of the pagans, and that it doesn't flow from the channel of justice derived from our fathers the patriarchs; we read about their funerals being celebrated; we don't read of funeral sacrifices being offered for them" (*serm.* 361.6). But he then rejects "the objection some people bring from the scriptures: 'Break your bread and pour out your wine on the tombs of the just, but do not hand it over to the unjust' (Tb 4:17)." The quote from the book of Tobit was apparently used by Christians seeking to show that scripture did in fact refer to the *parentalia* without criticism. Augustine rejects the literal interpretation and, because not all of his listeners were baptized, explains in veiled terms that the bread and wine must be understood allegorically as the body and blood of Christ. He finds support for his interpretation in the mention by the psalmist of "the just," taking this to mean that the text is concerned with the faithful, as opposed to "the unjust," the non-Christians, who were barred from participating in the Eucharist. Augustine can then conclude: "So nobody should try to turn a remedy into a hurt, and attempt to twist a rope from the scriptures, and with it lob a deadly noose over his own soul" (*serm.* 361.6). Again, beyond the warning and the lesson in exegesis, his comment makes it clear that there is agreement on the validity of the manner of argumentation. Needless to say, the principle that nonliteral exegesis can be applied to most Jewish scriptures complicates the search for specific rules of behavior in the scriptures.

Assuming that these Christians were of good faith, seeking rules of behavior in the scriptures was for them a way of defining themselves as Christian. The bishops could not, in principle, dispute the approach, but they nevertheless tried to control the argument on the basis of their exegetical expertise.

The Realm of God and the Realm of the Demons

In several sermons Augustine refutes an argument that he claims Christians use as a rationale to justify their behavior: the worship of God is for the sake of the kingdom of heaven, while for the sake of earthly benefits the devil or the demons are to be worshipped. This is the case, for instance, in a sermon where he explains Psalm 34 as an evocation of "God's help against enemies amid the tribulations of this world" (*in psalm.* 34.1.1). He introduces an objection: "There are people who say, 'God is good, great, supreme, invisible, eternal, incorruptible. He is to give us eternal life, and the incorruptibility that belongs to the life of resurrection; he has promised this. But secular and temporal interests are the province of demons, of the powers that rule this dark world'" (1.7). He then explains how this rationale is put to use: "By saying this, when they become bound by love for that sort of thing, they dismiss God as though he had no concern with them; and they attempt by illicit sacrifices, or various charms, or some forbidden inducement provided by men, to take care of their temporal needs—money, a wife, children, and all the other things they want, either as comforts for this life as it slips away, or to slow its onward march" (1.7). The division of the realms of power—eternal life for God, temporal life for the demons—is clearly presented here as a justification.

A similar development occurs in a sermon preached on Psalm 40. Augustine explains that the end of verse 3 ("May the Lord keep him safe and give him life, and render him blessed on earth") should make it clear that both eternal life and temporal help are God's gifts. Then he states: "There are plenty of bad Christians who pore over astrological almanacs, inquiring into and observing auspicious seasons and days. When they begin to hear themselves reproved for this by us, or by good Christians, better Christians, who demand why they meddle with these things, they reply, 'These precautions are necessary for the present time. We are Christians, of course, but that is for eternal life. We have put our faith in Christ so that he may give us eternal life, but the life in which we are engaged now does not concern him.' Not to put too fine a point on it, their argument could be briefly stated like this: 'Let God be worshipped with a view to eternal life, and the devil be worshipped for this present life'" (*in psalm.* 40.3). We see here that the justification offered by the "bad Christians" was prompted by the bishop, or other Christians who reproved their behavior, and that it included the strong claim that their own Christianness was simply not relevant in certain contexts.

The justification based on the division between eternal and temporal life should probably be taken as seriously by modern scholars as it was by Augustine himself, who seems to have preached against it many times.[8] However, Augustine's perspective on this distinction should not be adopted if we are to form an accurate picture of the Christians' understanding of Christianness. After all, he himself frequently calls their attention to the distinction between eternal and temporal life and admonishes them not to worship God for temporal benefits.[9] The practices that Christians justified with this principle fall in the category of magic, defined by Valerie Flint as "the exercise of a preternatural control over nature by human beings, with the assistance of forces more powerful than they" (1991: 3). Augustine mentions propitiatory prayers and/or sacrifices (*in psalm.* 26.2.19), astrology (40.3), the recourse to divination, the use of incantations and charms, the consultation of magi (34.1.7). However, rather than concluding that Christians continued old religious practices for which their new religion had no substitute, I would suggest that the division indicates contexts in which Christianness was not the principle on which Christians acted. Before we turn to texts in which we can see how Christians handled their different identities, we need to consider another distinction that Christians used as a justification.

Laypeople and Clergymen

While Augustine preached against the spectacles in the city of Bulla Regia, he raised the following objection: "It's all very well for you to abstain from these things, you clergy, you bishops, but not for us laypeople" (*serm.* 301A [Denis 17].8). These ecclesiastical categories, along with others, such as monks, appear in a number of other sermons, where Augustine always insists on the universal appeal of the Christian calling, with the implication that laypeople sometimes invoked categorizations that were irrelevant (*serm.* 73A [Caillau 2,5].3; 96.9; 114.4; 211.4). Regarding attendance at spectacles, Augustine's objectors probably argued that *laici* had social and civic obligations that clergy did not. Peter Brown also suggests that "the majority of Christians ... tended to deal with their own dilemmas at one remove, in the person of their leaders" (1998: 656). This finds confirmation in the rules preserved in the *Breuiarium Hipponense*, which records the decrees of the Council of Carthage in 397.[10] The behavior of the clergy and of their dependents had to meet high standards; for example, their sons could not attend spectacles (c. 11), they could not marry non-Catholics (c. 12), and their entire household had to be Christian before they could be ordained (c. 17). Since such strict regulations were imposed on their clergy, Christian laypeople thought that they themselves could enjoy more relaxed standards (Brown 1998: 655–658). Thus Christians defended the existence of different standards within the church and justified different behaviors under these standards.

These principles of justification are not merely excuses for backing away from exemplary behavior, as Augustine tends to present them. They reflect a nuanced understanding of Christianness, one that we also find evinced in the way Christians managed their multiple identities.

Christians and Their Multiple Identities

When Augustine imagines how Christians might be drawn to act in a way that he deems inappropriate to their faith, he frequently refers to their affiliations with groups whose constitutive principles are not, or are not primarily, those of Christianity; family, neighborhoods, and occupations are mentioned in such contexts. Augustine pushes this line of reasoning so far that he promotes Christians who adhere to their Christian identity as their unique principle of action to the status of martyrs.

Christians and "Local Communities"

In several sermons, Augustine reminds his audience that it is still possible to imitate the martyrs, and he gives examples of what he calls "martyrdom in time of peace" (see Rebillard 1994: 117–119). One recurring example particularly relevant to this study is that of the Christian on his sickbed who is invited to engage the services of a local ritual expert or to follow some traditional ritual practices (see Frankfurter 2002, for instance, for the taxonomy; Benseddik 1989 for the variety of medical practices in fourth-century North Africa).

A typical narrative is found in a sermon preached for the birthday of Protasius and Gervasius, the Milanese martyrs: "So while he's being wracked with pain, along comes trial and temptation by tongue; either some female, or a man, if man he can be called, approaches the sickbed, and says to the sick man: 'Tie on that spell, and you will get better; let them apply that charm, and you will get better. So-and-so, and So-and-so and So-and-so; ask, they all got better by using it.' He doesn't yield, he doesn't agree, he doesn't give his consent; he has to struggle, all the same. He has no strength, and he conquers the devil. He becomes a martyr on his sickbed, and he is crowned by the one who hung for him on the tree" (*serm.* 286.7). With the mention of the "So-and-sos," Augustine designates a group of persons familiar to the patient and his visitor, and he also implies that their relationship is not primarily based on their religious affiliation, but perhaps on family ties, on neighborhood, or on both. In this text Augustine does not say anything about the religious affiliation of the other persons, but the following two texts show that we cannot assume that Augustine believes that the characters involved in such scenarios are non-Christians.

The first text describes another sickbed scene: "You are lying on your sickbed, and are one of God's athletes. You can't move hand or foot, and you're fighting battles to the finish. The fever doesn't leave you, and your faith goes ahead to God. But lo and behold, a neighbor at your bedside, and a friend and a maid, even perhaps, as I said, your old nurse, bringing wax and an egg in her hand and saying, 'Do this and get better. Why prolong your illness? Tie on this amulet. I heard someone invoke the name of God and the angels over it, and you will get better. To whose care will you leave your widowed wife, to whose care your young children?' But he says, 'I won't do it, because I'm a Christian. Let me die in such a way that I don't thereby die forever'" (*serm.* 335D [Lambot 6].3). By mentioning prayers to God and the angels rather than incantations to the demons the old nurse presents the amulet as a more respectable remedy for a Christian.[11] It is not clear whether Augustine imagines her as a Christian or simply wants to suggest that she is aware that a Christian might refuse to tie an amulet to his body. In either case, the nurse suggests that the patient's roles as father and husband should take precedence over his Christianity in this specific situation.

The second text is a short allocution preached to the newly baptized. "Beware of the bad," admonishes Augustine. "You see, I know that bad people are going to come to you, and are going to try and persuade you to indulge in drunkenness, and they are going to say to you, 'Why not? Aren't we too very staunch believers?' Yes, I know they will, that's what saddens me, that's what I'm afraid of." And shortly after that: "Your neighbor, or his wife, is going to say to you, 'There's a good witch-doctor here, a good healer here, somewhere or other there's an astrologer.' What you say is, 'I'm a Christian, that sort of thing is forbidden to me.' And if he says to you, 'Why not? Am I not a Christian too?' you are going to say, "But I am one of the faithful.' And he will answer you, 'And I too have been baptized.' Members of Christ become the devil's angels" (*serm.* 376A.3). In this last case there is no doubt that the neighbors or friends are Christians. Augustine even imagines that they invoke their common membership so as to better seduce their fellows. The examples he sketches—drunkenness on the one hand, a visit to a local healer or an astrologer on the other—belong to very different spheres of interaction, even though Augustine stigmatizes them all as equally unfit for Christians. His rebukes suggest that there was a wide variety of situations in which Christians did not think their Christianness to be relevant.

Of course, what these texts illustrate best is Augustine's own opinion that one's Christian identity was the only identity of possible significance. We should not, therefore, infer too precise a social reality behind these scenarios. Nevertheless, they did need to sound plausible to his audience. In the text I examine next, the situation Augustine describes seems to reflect more specific tensions between the bishop and his congregation.

Christians and Their Patrons

In Sermon 62 preached in Carthage at a time when the temples were still open (Rebillard 2009a: 317 n. 80), Augustine tries to stop Christians from going to a pagan temple in order to please their superiors.

Among the readings chosen for that day was 1 Corinthians 8:10–12 on idol meat, a suitable scriptural text for admonishing Christians to stop participating in banquets held in temples. According to Augustine, some Christians believed that they could sit in a temple without breaking their faith because they knew that idols were mere stones. "Do you ever wonder how people may be led astray by images, when they think these are being honored by Christians?" he asks. To the objection "God knows my mind," he replies: "But your brother doesn't know your mind" (*serm.* 62.7). This is the argument with which Paul opposed the "strong" in 1 Corinthians: the "strong" know there is nothing intrinsically sinful about idol-meat eating, but the "weak" do not, and they might, consequently, be led astray.

But above all, these Christians excused their participation in the banquets as an obligation to a superior (*maior*):[12] "'But I'm afraid,' you will say, 'of offending a superior'" (*serm.* 62.8). Initially Augustine simply suggests: "See if there isn't perhaps one greater than the one you are afraid of offending" (8), but he soon returns to the argument and treats it at greater length. First, he invites Christians to consider their patrons' demands as a trial sent to them by God (12). Second, he makes it clear that he does not recommend contempt toward authorities, but rather invites the Christians to consider the higher authority of God (13). Third, he reminds his audience of the psalm sung during the service: "Like a sharp razor you have practiced deceit" (Ps 52:2). Just as a sharp razor can cause a man to fear for his neck, even though it will be used only to cut his hair, so the superior cannot deprive them of their life but only of superfluities (*serm.* 62.14).

Finally, Augustine compares his own age to the time of the persecutions: "The martyrs endured the butchery of their limbs, but will Christians dread the wrongs of a Christian age? The one who does you wrong now does it timidly. He doesn't say openly, 'Come to the idol.' He doesn't say openly, 'Come to my altars, join in the feast there.' And if he did say it, and you refused, let him make a formal complaint about it, let him prosecute you and put this complaint in his deposition: 'He refused to come to my altars, he refused to come to the temple where I worship.' Let him say that. Well of course, he doesn't dare say it, he has other deceitful tricks up his sleeve" (*serm.* 62.15). Augustine's point is that the superior cannot act as the persecutor had because Christians can no longer be legally constrained to worship idols.

We see how Augustine very skillfully equates an invitation to a banquet in a temple to an invitation to worship idols. However, we need not adopt his point of view about the relevance of religious affiliation in this context. The conventions at play in the interaction seem simply to have been those of the social obligations binding clients and patrons, and not specifically religious principles. In this case, the superior was probably actually honoring the Christian of Augustine's fictitious dialogue by inviting him to attend a banquet that he had organized, whether a public or a private feast. For our Christian, it seems that Christianness and, more generally, religious affiliation were not necessarily relevant to the situation, and the same was likely true for the patron. The fact that Augustine disagrees is another matter.

Christians and Civic Identity

The occasion of Sermon 62 might have been the celebration of the genius of Carthage, as an objection refuted by Augustine reveals. "'It isn't a god,' he says, 'it's the genius of Carthage.' As though if it were Mars or Mercury, it would be a god. But it's what they regard it as that counts, not what it is. I mean, I know as well as you do that it's only a stone. If a genius is some kind of distinction, then let the citizens of Carthage live well, and they will be the genius of Carthage" (*serm.* 62.10). The feast of the genius of Carthage was obviously an important event in the civic calendar (Lepelley 1992). Augustine clearly considers the feast a religious matter, while his comment that the genius is an *ornamentum* and his reference to the *cives Carthaginis* probably reflect his audience's point of view. Because the feast was, crucially, in honor of the genius of their city rather than one of the Greco-Roman deities ("Mars or Mercury"), some Christians (while they may not have necessarily considered it a secular event) likely viewed it simply as an event in which their participation was necessitated because they were citizens of Carthage. It appears, therefore, that they thought their Christianness was not of primary relevance in this context.

A sermon preached in Bulla Regia offers another good example of how, in the eyes of Christians, religious affiliation was not necessarily pertinent with respect to their civic identity. Augustine probably stopped in Bulla while returning from a trip to Carthage and was asked by the local bishop to speak on the topic of theatrical performances.[13] Not only was Bulla Regia famous for its spectacles, but it also, apparently, provided the whole region with actors and actresses. Augustine tries to shame the Christians of Bulla about their enthusiasm for the theater, and, in the course of his admonition, he refutes a potential objection: "But perhaps you will say: 'We are like

Carthage'" (*serm.* 301A [Denis 17].7). The objection is born of civic pride: "We are like Carthage" implies that Bulla was an important city, larger than Hippo or neighboring Simittu. Its citizens, therefore, looked to the example of Carthage when they thought of their status. Augustine's argument anticipates that Christians will excuse themselves through reference to the Jews and pagans who live in a big city such as Carthage: "Just as there is a holy and religious community in Carthage, so also there is such a vast population in a great metropolis, that they all use others to excuse themselves by. In Carthage, you can say: 'The pagans do it, the Jews do it'; here, whoever is doing it, Christians are doing it" (*serm.* 301A [Denis 17].7). We need not accept the implication that all the inhabitants of Bulla Regia at this time were, in fact, Christian. Augustine goes on to report that, in Simittu, when an imperial official organized a spectacle, none of the leading citizens attended. Further, he asks rhetorically: "Are they not decent people? Is that not a city? Is that place not a colony, and all the more decent, the emptier it is of these things?" (*serm.* 301A [Denis 17].9).[14] It is clear that what is at stake for the Christians of Bulla Regia is the status of their city and its standing among other North African cities. As is well known, spectacles were an important component of civic life, and this was still the case in Augustine's time (Lepelley 1979–81: vol. 1, 298–302; see Hugoniot 1996).

Christians and the Social Game

One last example is worth considering. In a sermon preached on the Calends of January 404 (Dolbeau 1996: 353–359), Augustine criticizes the Christians' participation in traditional celebrations (Scheid 1998) and, in particular, their exchange of gifts. The ritual of gift giving was conducted both among equals and between patrons and clients. It was a way of reaffirming the bonds of friendship and/or dependence all along the social scale (Meslin 1970: 76–77). Augustine invites his audience to give to the poor and introduces the following objection: "But you say to me, 'When I give good luck presents, I too receive them.'" Augustine's answer is, as expected, that gifts to the poor will be rewarded in a way incomparable with the presents that they would receive in the gift-giving ritual (*serm.* 198auct [Dolbeau 26].4). But the point of the exchange, for some of his listeners, was to participate in the larger social game, not to create a separate Christian community.

Arrangement of Category Membership Sets

I suggest that we can better understand the tensions we have observed in the texts here examined if we recall the distinction I presented in the introduction between two types of arrangement of category membership sets (see above, with reference to Handelman 1977). Through this model, these tensions can be understood as resulting from a conflict between hierarchical and lateral arrangements.

Augustine is clearly advocating for a hierarchical arrangement by which all membership sets are interpreted in terms of the religious set. "Christianness" should always be the most salient identity of Christians whenever and wherever they interact, whether with other Christians or with non-Christians. On the other hand, members of his audience display a preference for a lateral arrangement of membership sets in which situational selection is the principle. This means that other membership sets can be considered, in a given context, as having relevance equal to or greater than that of religion. In the sermons discussed above we have seen examples of situations in which Christians did not give salience to the religious set: when invited by a patron, they agreed to participate in ceremonies that could have been seen as forbidden to Christians; when civic pride was at stake, they gave it priority over their religious affiliation. Some letter exchanges preserved in Augustine's correspondence will allow us to examine in more detail how the two arrangements of membership sets can come into conflict and also to look more closely at the mechanisms of laterality and situational selection.

Letter Exchange and Identity Conflict

Four letter exchanges will be considered. The first three cases illustrate how Augustine strove to impose his own hierarchical arrangement of category membership sets on correspondents who did not share his point of view. Too often scholars have supposed that such a disagreement implied that the correspondent was a pagan. We will see that this conclusion is unsupported in all three cases. The last case is a rare example of a correspondent who successively gives salience to different category memberships in his interaction with Augustine.

Dioscorus

Dioscorus's letter exchange with Augustine was preserved in Augustine's library and is grouped with other letters under the label "Against Pagans" in the catalog made by Possidius (Wilmart 1931: 163).[15] However, this classification does not address Dioscorus's religious affiliation but is based, rather, on the content of Letter 118: its central section is a lengthy critical review of pagan philosophical doctrines.

Dioscorus was probably the brother of Augustine's longtime friend Zenobius. Whether or not Dioscorus and Augustine met while Dioscorus was studying in Carthage, his person and activities were well known to Augustine.[16] It was perhaps in the autumn of 410 (Perler 1969: 280–286), just before Dioscorus was to leave for Greece, that he sent Augustine a list of questions on the philosophical dialogues of Cicero. The list is lost, but not the short letter accompanying it (*epist.* 117) or the long answer written by Augustine (*epist.* 118). Because of his philosophical interests, some modern scholars have deemed Dioscorus a pagan (Wankenne 1974). However, Augustine clearly states that he knows Dioscorus prefers Christian teaching to all others and that he believes Dioscorus is "confident that it alone contains the hope of eternal salvation" (*epist.* 118.2.11), even though he warns Dioscorus against trying to "construct another way to reach and to gain the truth than that way which he [Christ] constructed who, as God, saw the weakness of our steps" (3.22).

Augustine's letter is not a rebuke to a pagan philosopher who, despite declared interest in Christianity, still lingers outside the church—he does not urge him to convert or to be baptized—but a rebuke to a Christian who does not orient all his intellectual interests according to his religion. Augustine also complains that Dioscorus has addressed him on the basis of his past status as a professor and intellectual, and not on the basis of his present status as bishop. Twice in his answer Augustine makes this clear: "It is not evident to me that there is nothing improper involved in this matter [Dioscorus's request]. For my mind fails to find a proper appearance of things when I think that a bishop, torn this way and that by noisy concerns of the Church, holds himself back from all these, as if suddenly become deaf, and explains minor questions about Ciceronian dialogues to a single student" (*epist.* 118.1.2). And again, with a clear allusion to his own past: "The basilica of the Christians at Hippo occurred to you as the place to deposit your concerns, because there now sits in it a bishop who once sold such ideas to children" (2.10). It is not so much the case that Augustine did not want to be reminded of his old self; what was at stake was a hierarchy of commitments. Augustine did, in fact, answer Dioscorus, even at considerable length, and he also returned the list of questions with annotations regarding the questions he did not address in his letter (5.34).

Dioscorus was not the only correspondent of Augustine to address him on the basis of his former identity, even though Augustine himself denied any salience to that identity once he had become a bishop. Augustine's social access to the representatives of imperial power, and to the Roman nobility more generally, was rather limited until 411–412, when he became friend with Marcellinus (McLynn 1999). However, even after this development, it was very often not because he was a Christian bishop, but because of his education and early career (on which see Lepelley 1987), that he was accepted as an interlocutor by members of the imperial elite, regardless of whether or not these acquaintances were themselves Christian.

Volusianus

Volusianus was residing in Carthage in 411–412 when he exchanged a few letters with Augustine.[17] Marcellinus very likely played an active role in this relationship, but Augustine was also known to Volusianus's mother and to his sister, Albina, the mother of Melania the Younger.[18] The women in the family were Christian, but Volusianus himself is generally presented as a pagan, and even one for whom paganism "seems to have been taken for granted" (Brown 1961: 7; see Chastagnol 1956).

The story of Volusianus's baptism on his deathbed is well known. When he was sent to Constantinople to arrange the marriage of Valentinian III and Eudoxia in 436, he wrote to his niece Melania the Younger, who decided to meet him in order to "save his soul" (Gerontius, *V. Melan.* 50). When Melania arrived, Volusianus was sick in bed, and she urged him to be baptized. When she hinted that she would talk to the emperors about the matter, Volusianus replied: "I exhort your holiness not to take from me the gift of self-determination with which God has honored us from the beginning. For I am completely ready and long to wash away the stain of my many errors" (53). Alan Cameron notes that this answer sounds like "the response of a catechumen rather than a pagan" (2011: 197). Indeed, a few days later, Melania is warned that her uncle might die a catechumen (Gerontius, *V. Melan.* 54) and, as the *Life* does not mention that he had became a catechumen since his arrival at Constantinople, we may suppose that he had been a catechumen for quite some time.[19] Whether Volusanius was a pagan more than twenty years earlier when he exchanged letters with Augustine, or a catechumen and hence a Christian, is difficult to determine.[20] This is, however, not as relevant as it might initially seem.

Augustine initiated the exchange with Volusianus. He invited him to read the scriptures and to ask as many questions as might arise. Augustine insisted that the exchange be conducted through letter writing since he wished to avoid the intrusion of "those who are not suited for such an undertaking and find more delight in contests of the tongue than in the enlightenment of knowledge" (*epist.* 132). Thus Augustine tried to establish with Volusianus a one-to-one relationship of the kind only a spiritual adviser could have with a seeker.

Volusianus took Augustine at his word and responded with some questions, but he proposed a very different script for their relationship. Indeed, Volusianus invited Augustine, in essence, to join a circle of friends who conversed variously depending on their talents and interests (*epist.* 135.1). No doubt these were other Roman aristocrats who held positions in Carthage and/or took refuge there after the sack of Rome (see Courcelle 1964: 58–67). One interest Volusanius mentions is rhetoric, saying: "I speak to someone who knows about that. For you also taught this a little before." And about poetry, he adds: "You do not leave even this part of eloquence unmentioned and without honor." Then, "the talk turned to philosophy," and again Volusianus adds: "You are familiar [with it] and accustomed to cultivate [it] with the talent of Aristotle and of Isocrates" (*epist.* 135.1). As we see, Volusianus took great care to remind Augustine that his credentials for admittance to such a circle were his education and early career.

As for the questions, Volusianus presented those of his friends rather than his own: "While our conversation delayed over these ideas, one of the many asked: 'And who is perfectly imbued with the wisdom of Christianity who can resolve certain ambiguous points on which I am stuck and can strengthen my hesitant assent with true or probable grounds for belief?'" Thus the mise-en-scène is very different from what Augustine had envisioned. So also is the following comment far from what he had expected to read: "It is a matter of interest for your reputation that I come to know the answers to my questions, because ignorance may somehow or other be tolerated in other priests without harm to the worship of God, but when it comes to Augustine, the bishop, whatever he may happen not to know is a failing in what is right" (*epist.* 135.2). In his answer Augustine did not fail to ask Volusianus to change his attitude toward him (*epist.* 137.1.3).

The two men were obviously trying to construct different scripts for their exchange. While Augustine considered faith to be primarily at stake and opposed rhetoric and learning to the simplicity of the scriptures, Volusianus insistently reinstated him to membership in the learned elite to whom religious affiliation was only secondary. Augustine invited him to meditate on the scriptures, but Volusianus expected answers to intellectual objections to Christianity raised in the sorts of contests that Augustine had rejected in advance as not being driven by "the enlightenment of knowledge" (*epist.* 132). Whether Volusianus was already a Christian or not at the time of this exchange, he did not want "religion" but rather a shared interest in learning to be the principle that organized his communication with Augustine.

Nectarius

Our next case is that of Nectarius,[21] whose religious affiliation has recently been questioned, although most scholars see him as a pagan.[22] He was the herald of the city of Calama and had begged Augustine for leniency after acts of violence against the church there in 408 (Hermanowicz 2004; 2008: 157–164). Nectarius was an old acquaintance of Augustine, and, although his father had been baptized, he himself had not—a fact Augustine teases him about (*epist.* 91.1–2). But it was Nectarius rather than his father who was involved in the replacement of the bishop of Calama in the late 390s (*epist.* 38.3; Mandouze and La Bonnardière 1982: 779; Hermanowicz 2008: 166–167), which indicates that he was at least a Christian, and probably a Catholic, even if not a faithful.

Nectarius, in a manner more befitting of a Christian than a pagan (*epist.* 90; Hermanowicz 2008: 167), reminds Augustine of the clemency to be expected from a bishop. When Augustine tells Nectarius how he received the pagans and listened to them in Calama, he does not associate Nectarius with them (*epist.* 91.10). Yet, when Augustine quotes Virgil, he calls him "the most famous poet in your literary tradition" (*epist.* 91.2; see again *epist.* 104.3; MacCormack 1998: 185–187), and he also appears to characterize Nectarius as an advocate for the allegorical interpretation of traditional poetry (*epist.* 91.5). Finally, Augustine's advice to Nectarius that, to truly flourish, the city should convert to the true God could be interpreted as implying that Nectarius too should convert (6). But Nectarius's answer leaves no doubt. He says that he approved of the way that Augustine, in his letter, attacked the worship of idols and the temple rituals and adds: "I was happy to listen, therefore, when you were pressing us towards the worship and religion of the most high God; I gratefully welcomed your invitation to look to the heavenly fatherland" (*epist.* 103.2). In fact, the rest of the letter reads precisely as if Nectarius were suggesting to Augustine that his own Christianity, even if he is not among the faithful, is just not relevant to their present discussion: "Though this city is to be sought and loved above all, I do not think that the other city in which we were born and raised should be abandoned" (2). It is Augustine who, again and again in his reply tries to cast the debate in terms of the binary opposition between pagans and Christians (see O'Donnell 2005: 188).

It is, therefore, quite likely that Nectarius was a catechumen in the Catholic Church. Jim O'Donnell describes him as "a perfectly ordinary Christian whose main allegiances are not religious but social" (2005: 185), and Neil McLynn calls him a "part-time pagan" (2009: 587). I suggest, rather, that Nectarius had multiple allegiances pertaining to different category membership sets (for instance, religious or civic), and that he did not act according to a fixed hierarchy between the sets but rather gave more salience to different sets according to context.

Nectarius wrote to Augustine not as a Christian, but as a leading citizen of Calama and also as an old acquaintance and a member of a shared culture. I do not think that we can infer that any display of religious allegiance was, to Nectarius's mind, displaced in the public sphere.[23] Its activation was probably considered appropriate in some interactions, but not in others. Bishops most likely believed that religious allegiance should be at the core of a person's identity, and so certainly did a number of Christians. However, we should not attribute the extreme opposite position to those who did not share the bishops' opinion: we need not imagine that, for them, religious allegiance was *always* less important than was social allegiance. In our last letter exchange, between Augustine and Macedonius, we can see how different category membership sets can be given intermittent precedence.

Macedonius

Almost nothing is known of Macedonius beyond what we learn from his letter exchange with Augustine.[24] Possidius mentions that he is vicar of Africa (*V. Aug.* 20), and the exchange of letters can be dated to 413–414, around the time of or soon after the publication of the first three books of the *City of God*, which Augustine sent to Macedonius (*epist.* 154.2). In a letter that has not been preserved, Augustine had asked Macedonius to grant a favor requested by the carrier of the letter, the bishop Bonifatius. From Macedonius's answer, we learn not only that the favor was granted, but also its nature: pardon for a criminal whose case he had judged (*epist.* 152.1–2). However, Macedonius had some reservations about the bishop's practice of interceding on behalf of criminals: "You say that it is the responsibility of your priesthood to intervene on behalf of the guilty and that you are offended if you do not get what you want, as if you did not get what pertains to your office. Here I have strong doubts that this comes from our religion" (2). It is obvious that Macedonius addresses the bishop Augustine as one Christian to another when he questions the religious grounds of intercession.

In his second letter, Macedonius does not comment on the long answer Augustine had written on the merits of intercession, but only notes the "respectfulness" Augustine displayed in his request: "For you do not insist that you obtain whatever you desire out of some concern—something that very many men of this place do. But you advise me of what you think you should ask for from a judge caught up in so many problems, and you use a respectfulness (*verecundia*) that among good men is most effective in difficult matters" (*epist.* 154.1; see Moreau 1998: 113–114). Macedonius not only reminds Augustine of his education and early career by placing him among the good men (*boni*), but he also makes it clear that, when it comes to the granting of favors, he himself will act not as a Christian who defers to the bishop, but as a magistrate who will honor the *amicitia* of another member of his social group, if that member knows the rules of the game. The respectfulness Macedonius praises may also have been intended to remind Augustine of the imperial magistrate's superiority over the bishop (so Moreau 1998: 113), but Augustine, who did not fail to pick up on Macedonius's reference to *verecundia*, warns him that all the efforts exerted in administering his office are futile with regard to the truly happy life (*epist.* 155.3.10). In this way Augustine shows that it did not escape his attention that Macedonius did not intend to use "religion" as a principle in governing his administration, and he rebukes him for this, even—as he says in substance (3.11)—at risk of being disrespectful.

In Augustine's letter exchange with Macedonius we see an unambiguous example of how one person can give salience to different category membership sets in his various interactions—and even in the course of one interaction if we view the letter exchange, which seems to have been limited to the letters we have discussed, as a single interaction—with the same person. When Macedonius wrote his first letter to Augustine, his Christianness was the category that was given salience: he wanted to understand, as a Christian, why the bishop thought it his duty to intercede on behalf of guilty criminals. In his second letter he advises Augustine that religion will not be relevant or at least not given salience over other category memberships in the administration of his office.

I contend that the evidence, both sermons and letters, confirms that a lateral arrangement of category membership sets, which accommodates situational choices, is a more adequate model for understanding the behavior of Christians at the time of Augustine. It is quite obvious that a hierarchical arrangement of category membership sets, in which Christianness is the guiding principle in all contexts, is not the arrangement embraced by all Christians. However, the tensions highlighted in Augustine's sermons and letters are not tensions between two different hierarchical arrangements (one that privileges religious affiliation, and another privileging one of the other membership sets).[25] As we have seen, just as we cannot assume that Christianness was always activated and given salience, or even significance, simply because it was available as a category membership, so also we need to understand that other category memberships were, just like Christianness, given salience only intermittently.

Christians and Groupness

Once the presumption of the unique relevance of religious affiliation has been abandoned, we need to study how Christianness worked as a basis for group-formation. The most obvious context for such a study is the series of events that have been construed as episodes of a fundamentally religious conflict between "pagans" and "Christians." The traditional narrative holds that, in North Africa at the turn of the fifth century, relations between pagans and Christians became particularly tense and were marked by a series of violent episodes (Chadwick 1985: 11–13; Markus 1990: 112–118). The cause of these new tensions is said to be imperial legislation, which became most extreme in the 390s. In North Africa specifically, in 399 Honorius dispatched to Carthage two emissaries, Gaudentius and Jovius, with the order to destroy temples and statues. This mission is credited with fostering a wave of iconoclastic rage among Christians, who went through the countryside looking for cultic statues to destroy (see, most recently, Oliveira 2006: 245–246). The significance of Gaudentius and Jovius's mission has been greatly exaggerated by modern scholars. As I show elsewhere, it went quite unnoticed at the time, and Augustine refers to the event only once, nearly a quarter of a century later, when he found it mentioned in a consular list he had consulted for purposes of disproving a pagan prediction (*ciu.* 18.54, with Rebillard, forthcoming). However, a number of episodes, though somewhat arbitrarily clustered around 399 by modern scholars (Rebillard 2009a and forthcoming), undeniably attest to tensions and even violence. What I intend, however, is to analyze these episodes without taking for granted that Christians (or "pagans" for that matter) constantly activated their group identity, and consequently to understand how groupness happened.

Sufes

At Sufes, a small Roman colony in Byzacena (Lepelley 1979–81: vol. 2, 305–307), a statue of Hercules was destroyed under circumstances that are difficult to establish. The episode is known through a letter that Augustine addresses to the authorities of the colony, in which he mocks their request that the statue be restored, contrasting the fact that sixty Christians had been killed and their murderers left unpunished (*epist.* 50).[26] Augustine is eloquent on the savagery of the citizens of Sufes and the indifference or even collusion of the municipal authorities, but he gives no indications of the circumstances of the destruction itself. Even though a considerable number of Christians were killed, there is no mention, in particular, of whether the statue had been destroyed by a Christian mob or even a group of Christians rather than by an individual.

Indeed, several elements in the letter concur to suggest that the destruction was the responsibility of the local clergy. First, Augustine indicates that the municipal authorities had contested the legality of the destruction: "If you pretend that the Hercules was yours, we will give it back to you." Second, his mockery of the statue's golden and jewelry ornaments also suggests that the authorities might have evoked the imperial laws protecting statues for their artistic value (on this legislation, see Lepelley 1994). A discussion of the legal context of the destruction does not suggest the action of a raving mob. Augustine's intervention and the fact that he mentions his position as bishop in the address of the letter imply, finally, that the clergy of the colony was directly involved. All these elements suggest that the local clergy thought they had the right to proceed with the destruction of the statue. The pogrom that followed is no less difficult to interpret. The Christians were undeniably categorized as a group and targeted by the local inhabitants, but we know too little of the circumstances for further analysis.[27]

Calama

It is interesting to compare the incident described above with the events at Calama in 408. The details of the Calama riots are known through Augustine's letter exchange with Nectarius, the local noble of his acquaintance whom we met already (*epist.* 91.8; see Hermanowicz 2004: 484–486 for a reconstruction of the events; also 2008: 157–164). On June 1, 408, a procession, which was part of the annual celebration held on the Calends of June, was about to pass by the doors of the Christian basilica when the clerics attempted to halt it. The church was stoned in retaliation. It was stoned again a week later, when the bishop Possidius tried to make a formal complaint, and again the following day, after Possidius had insisted that the municipal authorities supply protection for the church. On this day, the church was also set on fire, and the clerics pursued through the town, and one of them was even killed in the street. It is worth noting that Augustine describes the acts of violence in the passive voice, avoiding explicit reference to the perpetrators. Indeed, even if he designates the feast of the Calends of June as a "feast of the pagans" (*festo paganorum*), he does not comment on the religion of the participants in the procession. The celebrants might well have included both Christians and non-Christians (see Hermanowicz 2004: 485 on the nature of the annual festival). It has often been noted that lay Christians are conspicuously absent from Augustine's narrative, with the exception of a stranger who attempted to rescue the members of the local clergy (*epist.* 91.8–9; Hermanowicz 2004: 485). It looks as though Possidius and his clergy were rather isolated in their position, and Nectarius, as we saw above, seems to have been a Christian himself, even if only a catechumen. Thus, the Christians of Calama were not mobilized, even to defend their bishop, and whatever the exact nature of the groupness provoked among Calama's denizens by Possidius's initiative, it is not obvious that it was based on religious affiliation.[28]

Carthage

Two sermons that were preached in Carthage by Augustine on two successive Sundays, possibly in 401, are particularly relevant to a discussion of the mechanisms of groupness.[29]

THE SHAVING OF HERCULES

The first sermon was preached by Augustine after a statue of Hercules had been mutilated in circumstances that he does not describe. Indeed, he did not need to tell his audience what had happened. A recent study of the incident proposes that the governor, tentatively identified as a pagan,[30] first gave his authorization for the regilding of the statue of Hercules, and then, under pressure from the Christian crowd, ordered the golden beard to be removed (Oliveira 2006: 252–254). However, this attempt to provide a coherent explanation of the governor's actions takes Augustine's sarcastic remark too seriously when he says that the governor did not authorize the regilding of the statue in order to compel Christians to adore the idol, but so that a Christian could mutilate it (*serm.* 24.6). Similarly, it is unlikely that the governor had sought to humiliate the (pagan) municipal authorities who made the request,[31] and we can, therefore, eliminate the possibility that the governor had planned the "shaving" of the statue before the event. Augustine's purpose is more likely to insinuate that the governor's decision to authorize the regilding of the statue could be presented to the imperial authorities as an anti-Christian measure. He is trying, in this way, to exert pressure on the governor so that the act of mutilation may go unpunished.

Augustine's intentions were similar when he roused the acclamations of the Christians assembled in the church earlier in the sermon (*serm.* 24.4–5). There is no evidence that the acclamations of the crowd in the church were a spontaneous continuation of gatherings that would have taken place in the streets of Carthage earlier the same day (*contra* Oliveira 2006: 247). In fact, Augustine had very deliberately provoked his audience to shout for the destruction of the statues. The beginning of the sermon comments on the first two verses of Psalm 82, which had been sung during the service.[32] In order to explain verse 1 ("God, who is like you?"), Augustine compares the faithful to the living stones of the temple of God (*serm.* 24.1) and opposes them to the dead stones, which are not the statues of the false gods, but the men who adore such stones (2). Indeed, Augustine suggests that even some Christians are not immune of some form of adoration, since they may be quite content to read the inscription "To Hercules the god" on the base of a statue. To read such a title is dangerous, as "it imposes the name of a god as a fiction on a fiction, and deletes the name of a worshipper from the book of the living" (3). He then introduces verse 2 ("Do not keep quiet or grow gentle, God"), recognizing that this appeal might seem contradictory to Christ's general kindness, and then inviting his audience to concentrate their attention on this difficulty (4). At this point Augustine is interrupted by some acclamations, one of which he later repeats: "As at Rome so at Carthage" (6). What has happened is clear: the people assembled in the church have called for the destruction of the statues. Augustine congratulates them for their zeal, but he recommends that they let their bishops act: "We have tried and tested you. Now it's your turn to try and test us, to see if after these voices which have borne witness to your thoughts and your keenness we are slack in doing what ought to be done" (5). Clearly Augustine does not invite his audience to initiate some sort of "collective action," but neither does he try to cool their iconoclastic rage. It seems, rather, that he purposefully aroused their acclamations: as he says, they passed the test successfully by shouting when he mentioned that Christian hearts were quite content to read statue titles such as "To Hercules the god." The example, needless to say, was not chosen casually.

The acclamations of the audience along with the message of Augustine himself were, no doubt, reported to the governor.[33] However, there is no evidence that a Christian "mob" was responsible for the mutilation.[34] There is also no mention of gatherings outside the church, and therefore no reason to understand this episode as an outburst of violence that was part of a series of Christian attacks against pagan statues. It is certainly the case that Augustine fostered some level of groupness among his audience on this precise day, and it is also very likely that he deployed this unity, directly or indirectly, in his interactions with the governor. The fact that groupness was initiated by the bishop does not necessarily mean that it was confined to the space of the church and the duration of the sermon. Indeed, it is not impossible that the "shaving" episode had some connection with the affair reported in the second sermon (a tentative suggestion of Oliveira 2006: 259).

THE CONVERSION OF FAUSTINUS

On the following Sunday, Aurelius, the bishop of Carthage, asked Augustine to talk to his congregation about the conversion of Faustinus, a prominent pagan, and Augustine appropriately decided to preach a sermon on the conversion of Paul. At the end of the sermon he introduced the convert to the congregation and asked them to welcome him despite their doubts about his sincerity. Indeed, Faustinus was a banker (*argentarius*), and he was running either for the office of *curator rei publicae*, the "mayor" of the city, or that of *exactor*, the local who was foremost responsible for tax collection (Oliveira 2006: 259). Faustinus had been the object of negative acclamations from the Christians because of his declared hostility to the church. Whichever he was seeking, both offices were granted by the governor, and acclamations were therefore part of the usual nomination process (260). Now, the congregation suspected that Faustinus's conversion was merely strategic, that is, pursued only to guarantee an easier nomination. Augustine does not deny the possibility but insists that only God can read Faustinus's heart (*serm.* 279.10).

It can only be speculated when the acclamations took place,[35] but it is clear that they were shouted in the church and apparently under the bishop's control, or at least with his approval. Indeed, Augustine recalls that both clergy and lay congregation had put up a common front against Faustinus before his conversion: "We bishops didn't plan and set up what has happened, because we didn't even have any hopes of it; both your and our intention was quite different. You know what cry was raised here, you know it well: Pagans should not be *maiores*! Pagans should not have authority over Christians!" (*serm.* 279.12). It seems that this was another instance of the bishop using his congregation as an instrument of political pressure.

Augustine could mobilize his audience for the duration of his preaching, and he was aware that the effects of this mobilization sometimes extended beyond the church. However, he also knew all too well that, once outside the church, some members of his audience might deactivate, so to speak, their Christianness. He thus concluded the sermon on the conversion of Faustinus by reminding his audience of the feast of John the Baptist on the following day, and by urging them not to join the non-Christians, for whom it was also a holiday (*serm.* 279.13).

In sum, there is no good evidence that the incidents we have reviewed involved the opposition of clear-cut and stable groups, despite Augustine's presentation and his use of the categories "pagan" and "Christian." Augustine did succeed in mobilizing his audience to act as a Christian group, for instance through their acclamations. However, these instances offer no evidence that Christians acted as a group whose basis was Christian membership when the service was over and they had left the church. The rare documented cases of actual destruction of statues were not the work of unleashed Christian mobs but were carefully orchestrated by the bishop and his clergy.[36]

It seems that heated religious rhetoric was not especially compelling or that, when it was, its effects were limited.[37]

Conclusion

If we do not adopt Augustine's point of view and instead pay attention to the points of view he opposes, we come to realize that Christianness was not the common frame of interpretation for everyday experience. More importantly and more innovatively, we also see that Christians themselves assumed exactly this situation and were able, when challenged, to justify themselves. An acute awareness of the issues related to handling category membership sets is displayed in our evidence. These conclusions invite us to look beyond the separation of the religious and the secular that has become axiomatic in the field of late antique studies (Markus 1990; see Rebillard and Sotinel 2010). Indeed, the division between the religious and the secular is typical of a hierarchical arrangement of category membership sets, while, as my analysis suggests, a lateral arrangement tended to prevail among Christians.

One corollary of an approach that makes room for the internal plurality of individuals is the establishment of the group-making process as an object of study (as opposed to the assumption of groups and their treatment as actors). From this perspective I have reconsidered events traditionally described as episodes of Christian violence against pagans in North Africa at the turn of the fourth to the fifth century, and I have shown that Christians responded positively to their bishop's efforts to mobilize them. But, beyond the limited effects of such mobilization, there was no evidence that Christians constantly thought of themselves as a group opposed to another group in the everyday life of their city.

Transferring our unit of analysis from the group to the individual thus yields some important results and invites us to begin rethinking some of the general assumptions we share about the period.

Conclusion

That Christianness did not define early Christians' experience in all of their interactions is not in itself an unexpected conclusion. Nevertheless, I think that it has been fruitful to focus specifically on the intermittency of Christian religious identity, as this has typically been underemphasized in early Christian studies. In the preceding chapters, my goal was not to show that Christians enjoyed "normal" day-to-day relations with non-Christians (a point conceded by most scholars of early Christianity), but to argue that Christianness was only one of a plurality of identities available to be activated in a given situation (a point too often neglected in favor of the study of group or collective identity).

Christians and Their Many Identities

I have not followed Tertullian or Augustine when they imposed, through their very selective focus, Christianness as the interpretive framework for everyday situations. Instead I have tried to determine the circumstances under which Christians invoked Christianness as the guiding principle of their behavior. It appears that Christians were aware of the issues associated with handling multiple identities and that religion was given salience only intermittently, as was also the case with their other category membership sets. I have not attempted to systematically map the contexts in which Christianness was used as a principle of action. Not only would evidence be lacking for such a project, but the undertaking would necessarily assume a consistency among and within individuals that cannot be taken for granted.

Just as Christianness was given salience only intermittently in everyday experience, groupness based on Christianness also occurred only intermittently, and Christians could be involved in groupness that was not based on Christianness. When I looked for contexts in which Christianity was the principle of group-formation, I not only found very few, but I also concluded that instances of groupness did not necessarily last. This does not mean that it needed to be reconstituted each time it occurred. That is to say, the fundamental intermittency and the episodic character of Christianness should not be understood as necessarily in contradiction to the existence of a strong group identity, and bishops did succeed in constructing Christian identity as that of a bounded group. However, while this identity was available, it was not necessarily activated.

The intermittency of Christianness must not be interpreted, therefore, as a measure of its importance or even of its significance. I would like to emphasize that, in the end, my argument is not about how much or how little religion, in our case Christianity, matters, but about how religion worked for Christians in late antiquity.[1] As evinced in the case of North Africa, religion and religious affiliation were neither the unique nor even the primary principles of action for Christians.

Religious Pluralism

At this point the question arises of what features, in terms of the workings of religion, differentiate the period under consideration. The answer lies partly in the development of religious pluralism.

Religious pluralism, while not unknown previously (see Bendlin 2000), nevertheless achieved an unprecedented scale in the second century (North 1992; 2000: 63–75; North talks about a "religious revolution"). I would suggest that this new prevalence of religious pluralism made individuals more aware of issues related to handling different category membership sets, especially as it brought into play a set—the religious set—that was previously absent. Jörg Rüpke shows that, though there was no theory of religious plurality, "a space of communication" had been newly opened (2010: 761). Daniel Boyarin goes further and notes that "the system of identities had been completely transformed during the period extending from the first to the fifth centuries," and describes the introduction of "religious difference as a modality of identity" as a "systemic change" (2009: 19).

Boyarin also emphasizes that Judaism was not a "religion" before the mid-third century, when the term *Ioudaismos/Iudaismus* came to mean "Judaism" (2009:11; see Mason 2007). It is no accident that the Mishnah tractate *Avodah Zarah* is contemporary with Tertullian's *De idololatria* and that the two texts are often compared by scholars.² As Seth Schwartz has shown, the "rabbis who did live in the cities and wished to win the support of their Jewish inhabitants, whose religious behavior and thought in many cases differed in no way from those of the pagans ... needed to develop a mechanism to allow them to live in the cities and to participate in some of the cities' public activities, pagan though they were" (2001:164). The rabbis limited idolatry to the cultic aspect of paganism and "declared the noncultic, but still religious, aspects of urban culture acceptable" (164; see, more generally, 162–176). This "mechanism" recalls some of the discussions Tertullian (see chapter 1) and Augustine (see chapter 3) attest to among Christians in North Africa.

Thus the answer to the question about the specificity of the period is that it saw the development of religious pluralism and the appearance of "religion," a notion that is usually associated with modernity (see, for instance, Asad 1993: 40–42). Whether it "was virtually dropped, to lie dormant for a thousand years" after having been "invented" (or at least approached at a conceptual level) in late antiquity, as has been suggested by Wilfred Cantwell Smith (1963: 28), is not a question we can decide here.³

Abandoning Old Paradigms

Our new understanding of how religion and religious affiliation worked for Christians in late antiquity suggests that we need to abandon some old paradigms.

"Semi-Christians"

One approach that is often criticized but nevertheless lingers in academic discourse is the use of the category "semi-Christian" for describing Christians who did not fully embrace Christianity.⁴ When Charles Guignebert introduced the label in 1923, he wanted to bridge the gap that was too often thought to separate definitively the old and the new religion. He also wished to explain the ease of Christianization by pointing out the existence of numerous people who in fact had a "double religious life." Guignebert intended to distinguish the semi-Christians from Christians who adapted pagan practices to their new faith, and from those who were bad Christians and could not meet their new obligations. Among the pre-Constantinian examples discussed by Guignebert is the case of Martialis, a Spanish bishop, who had recourse to a *collegium* for the burial of his sons, and also the numerous Christian epitaphs that use the traditional dedication formula to the Manes (1923: 77, 79).

German scholars use the category "halben Christen" in a looser way to describe the phenomenon of mass Christianization,[5] as does Gerald Bonner, who popularized the category "semi-Christian" in English in his paper on the extinction of paganism (1984). Bonner was looking for a "deeper psychological factor" in addition to state coercion and the influence of powerful patrons in order to explain mass conversion (348). According to Bonner's analysis, the semi-Christians constituted the reservoir from which the church drew many of its converts after the Constantinian revolution (350–355). Although he concedes that there were semi-Christians before the Peace of the Church, he notes that their number increased considerably afterward: "The negative effect on the Church of the passing away of paganism was the dilution of the quality of Christian living brought about by an influx of converts with a semi-Christian outlook" (355).

Recently, a more radical departure from the dichotomy between pagans and Christians has been thought necessary. Thus Maijastina Kahlos proposes that we replace the category of semi-Christians with a new category of her own, that of the *incerti* (2007: 26–28 for a criticism of the dichotomy, and 30–34 for the *incerti*; see also 2004), while Alan Cameron suggests "as many as five overlapping categories": at the two extremes, committed pagans and committed Christians; then, center-pagans on one side and center-Christians on the other; in the middle, a large group of people that "resisted straightforward classification" (2011: 176–177).

All these attempts to refine the dichotomy between pagans and Christians continue to give unique relevance to a singular classification.[6] We saw that religious affiliation was given salience only intermittently and that it had no unique relevance in determining Christians' behavior. Thus the issue cannot be reduced to a question of level of commitment or degree of conversion. When we take into account the fact that individuals hold multiple identities, we are led to abandon derogatory categories of analysis, whether they be semi-Christians, center-pagans, or *incerti*.

The Religious and the Secular

In *The End of Ancient Christianity*, Robert Markus rightly rejects the use of categories such as semi-Christians, because it is not clear who makes "judgments about the extent of conversion" (1990: 8). Instead, Markus looks for "the manner in which Late Roman Christians, lay and clerical, drew the line which distinguished what they would have seen as their 'religion' from the rest of their activity and experience, their 'secular' lives and its settings" (15). Such a goal might initially seem very similar to the one pursued here, to determine how and when Christianness mattered.

One example given by Markus is that of the observances of the New Year celebrations. He writes that lay congregations considered them "harmless customs without religious significance" (1990: 14; see 107–123 more generally on secular festivals in Christian times).[7] However, by introducing the notion of "religious significance," the modern historian adopts the point of view of the bishops, who constantly forced the distinction between religious and secular on their congregations. Indeed, it is crucial to distinguish between the availability of a category membership and its activation. The audiences addressed by both Tertullian and Augustine did not neatly separate their activities and experiences into those that were "religious" and those that were "secular," unless challenged to do so. Rather, they decided on a situational basis when Christianness mattered in their activity and experience. We should, therefore, avoid replacing the dichotomy between "Christian" and "pagan" with a dichotomy between "religious" and "secular."[8]

Opening Up New Questions

In the dominant narrative, the "Constantinian revolution" continues to be presented as the great divide in the history of Christianity. One aspect of the "cataclysmic change" it brought to Christians is mass Christianization, and with it came the fourth-century "crisis of identity." In Markus's words (1990: 31), "mass-Christianization of Roman society from the highest level down [deprived] Christians of a clearly felt and easily discernible identity in their society." With the Peace of the Church, Christians are said to have lost the sense of belonging to an externally bounded group. I contend, however, that the intermittency of Christianness is structurally consistent in the everyday life of Christians from the end of the second to the middle of the fifth century. Thus the sense of belonging was just as available and just as often—or infrequently—activated in Augustine's time as it was in Tertullian's. If mass Christianization did not change the way religion works for Christians, we are then led to ask whether the notion of a "crisis of identity" should in fact be considered an element of the "narrative" or "representation" of Christianization generated by Christian bishops at the turn of the fifth century. As Peter Brown suggests, the narrative of Christianization should be understood as an issue of authority for the bishops and their congregations (1995: 23–24).

CONCLUSION

The preceding considerations show that a broader and more systematic comparison of the pre-Constantinian and Theodosian periods is needed. While noting that such a comparison is too rarely conducted, Michel-Yves Perrin also remarks that the similarities in clerical discourse on dissimulation and hypocrisy from these two periods invalidate its use as evidence for levels of religious allegiance (2010: 58, 60–61). A careful reading of both Tertullian's treatises and Augustine's sermons and letters shows that for Christians the issue is not the intensity of their religious allegiance, but its salience in the different arenas of their everyday life. On both sides of the "Constantinian divide," Christians practiced a similar and deliberate situational selection of the category membership set that would determine their behavior, and they did not necessarily give salience to Christianness.

A new set of questions also arises about the specificity of Christianity in the marketplace of religions in the late Roman Empire. It has often been assumed that belonging to an internally homogeneous and externally bounded group was an essential definitional component of Christianity (see Stowers 2011 for a recent criticism of this assumption). While my findings do not necessarily question this assumption, they do emphasize that this identity was only intermittently activated. We should, then, from this new perspective, reexamine our assumptions about what made Christians want to be Christian.

 Notes

Introduction

1. Elizabeth A. Clark has been instrumental in this regard: see Clark 1998, 2004; see also Martin and Cox Miller 2005.

2. Such books in English include Kraemer 1992; White 1996; Gregg and Urman 1996; Edwards 1996; Edwards et al. 1999; Hopkins 1999; Janowitz 2001; and Aviam 2004.

3. I use the rare "Christianness" instead of "Christianity," as it has a more limited range of uses and simply means "the Christian quality" (*OED* 1989, 2nd ed., s.v. "Christianness").

4. This methodological shift should be viewed in the context of the sociological exploration of the relationship between social structure and individual agency. See Adams 2006 for a review of theories that try to hybridize the notion of self-reflexivity, associated with the work of Anthony Giddens (1991), and that of "habitus," associated with the work of Pierre Bourdieu (1977, 1990, 2000). Lahire (2004: 695 ff.) offers a thorough criticism of Durkheim's suspicion about the individual actor and reviews its consequences for the development of sociology.

5. On identity theory, see Burke and Stets 2009. A less quantitative approach is proposed in McCall and Simmons 1966 and 1978.

6. A shared assumption among specialists of religion in the ancient world is that ancient personalities differ from modern personalities with their individualistic tendencies, and, as a consequence, scholars usually emphasize collective identities. See, for instance, Harland (2009: 7), who makes reference to the "dyadic or group-oriented nature of ancient personalities." However, as shown by Spiro (1993), one must not confuse a normative cultural conception of the self with the experience of the self by the actors.

7. However, see Edwards (2004), who dates the writing of the *Adversus nationes* to 326–327 rather than to 303–305, as usually assumed; on Arnobius, see Simmons 1995.

8. I do not offer anything close to a full treatment of material culture for the fourth and fifth centuries. On the one hand, most of the evidence relevant to the kind of questions I address would be related to death and burial, an area I did not wish to revisit (see Rebillard 2009b). On the other hand, the fact that the same artifacts were enjoyed by both pagan and Christian aristocrats has been emphasized many times (see, for instance, Brown 1995: 12 ff.).

Chapter 1

1. See Barnes 1985: 3–29, 245–247, with Braun 1972; Dunn 2004: 3–11, which also provides a description of Tertullian's works.

2. I use the proportion of one-thirtieth of the total urban and metropolitan population rather than 0.35 percent of the total population as we have good reasons to think that more Christians were living in cities than not, and I would also add that their presence was proportionally even greater in the larger cities than in the small. Tabbernee (2001: 380–381) uses the 0.35 percent figure and a population for Carthage of about 90,000 inhabitants and thus arrives at a total of 300 to 400 Christians in Carthage at the time of Tertullian. Carthage with 70,000 inhabitants (instead of older higher estimates of 300,000) can still be considered a metropolis: see Gros 2000; Picard 1990: 155–160.

3. For the *Apologeticum*, I use the Latin text of Jean-Pierre Waltzing (Paris, 1914); my translations are based on that of T. R. Glover, Loeb Classical Library 250 (Cambridge, MA, 1931).

4. The reconstruction of the early Christian gatherings is the object of a number of polemics that we need not enter into here. Tertullian does not specify on what day the evening gathering took place (*apol.* 39), but it is usually assumed to have been on Sunday. See McGowan 2004 and Alikin 2010 for an up-to-date *status quaestionis*.

5. By the time of Cyprian, the morning gathering was the most significant, and it was also the meeting at which the whole group was theoretically present: see McGowan 2004 and Alikin 2010: 98–99.

6. See Petropoulou 2008: 99–102 for a challenge to Rives's statement with (little) evidence for the Greek East. As far as I know there is no parallel evidence on mandatory individual participation to sacrifice in Africa.

7. I use the Latin text of Marie Turcan, Sources Chrétiennes 332 (Paris, 1986); my translations are based on that of T. R. Glover, Loeb Classical Library 250 (Cambridge, MA, 1931). I am also greatly indebted to Marie Turcan's introduction and notes.

8. Van Der Nat (1964) points out the importance of the assertions of opponents: "The treatise is a debate from beginning to end" (143). Turcan (1986: 28–37) convincingly shows that the objections do not provide a structure to the treatise. However, they remain a crucial element, and they need to be examined closely.

9. On Tertullian and the "silence" of scripture, see O'Malley 1967: 129–134.

10. In *coron.* 6.3 the *suaviludii* are associated with a treatise on public shows written in Greek: see Turcan 1986: 45.

11. I use the Latin text of Marie Turcan, Sources Chrétiennes 173 (Paris, 1971); my translations are based on that by S. Thelwall, Ante-Nicene Fathers 4 (New York, 1885). On the composition of the treatise, see Braun 1966.

12. I use the Latin text, English translation, and commentary of J. H. Waszink and J. C. M. Van Winden, Supplements to Vigiliae Christianae 1 (Leiden, 1987).

13. However, as Philip Harland has shown, this custom was less specifically Christian than is usually assumed by scholars, since a number of different associations used sibling language to express belonging (2009: 63–81).

Chapter 2

1. With a few exceptions, such as Giovannini 1984 (see also Giovannini 1996) for a "Neronian" persecution and Frend and his followers for a "Severan" persecution (see Daguet-Gagey 2001 for the bibliography).

2. The legal basis for persecution has generated a huge amount of scholarship, but I will make no attempt to summarize it; see, for instance, Engberg 2007: 71–73.

3. As underlined recently by Jakob Engberg, there has been very little debate regarding "private opposition" to Christians (2007: 77–79).

4. The first two volumes of Monceaux 1901–23 are still fundamental; Barnes (1985: 143–163; see also 2010: 43–96) and Birley (1992) provide a thorough and up-to-date presentation of the evidence.

5. The most thorough attempt at counting martyrs in North Africa is Y. Duval 1982: 483–492. For the persecutions of the pre-Constantinian period, no inscription records martyrs that are not known through literary sources (485). The only conclusion reached is that, though "considerable," the number of martyrs cannot be established (484).

6. However, although there is no positive evidence, it is also possible that Candidus was proconsul of Africa shortly before 193 and had processed the case in this capacity (Birley 1992: 44 n. 51).

7. I leave aside the case of Mavilus of Hadrumetum. Barnes (1985: 267–269) sees him as a victim of Scapula in 212; Birley (1991), as a victim of Caecilius Capella, who would have been proconsul of Africa between 184 and 188 or between 191 and 193. See Dunn 2005 with new arguments in favor of this latter interpretation.

8. As Baxter proved definitively, the martyrs of Madauros mentioned in the correspondence of Augustine are Donatists martyrs (1924; see Barnes 1985: 261–262; Mastandrea 1985: 27–31); the epithet "archimartyr" is a mockery of Maximus, not an allusion to some African "protomartyrs."

9. On the dating and order of writing, see Braun 1978: 222–231.

10. I cannot discuss fully Anne Daguet-Gagey's (2001) elaborate theory, in which she reconciles contradictory evidence on the role of Septimius Severus in the persecutions of Christians during his reign. She dates to 197 the legislation of Severus on *collegia* (*Dig.* 47.22.1) and suggests that it put Christians in the position of being accused of forming illegal associations.

11. Our only source on these events is the *Passio of Perpetua and Felicitas*. For a good up-to-date discussion of this text and the many historical problems attached to it, see Kraemer and Lander 2000; see Amat 1996 for a convenient edition of both the Latin and the Greek versions and also of the later Acts; and Musurillo 1972: 106–131 for the standard English translation.

12. Rives (1996: 22–23) does not mention the last two appearances of the crowd in the *Passion*. On the topic of popular hatred, Amat (1998; on *Pass. Perp.*, see 295–297) is very naive. A more nuanced analysis is found in Engberg 2007: 277.

13. See *Pass. Perp.* 5.6, where the father is the only one who does not rejoice in her martyrdom; 20.10 for the brother.

14. Two Carthaginians, Castus and Aemilius, are sometimes supposed to have suffered initially in 203, when they failed to bear testimony, and then endured martyrdom in 250 (Cyprian, *laps.* 13; Monceaux 1901–23: vol. 1, 45; Y. Duval 1982: 726). Clarke (1973a: 656–657) suggests that the two incidents in which they face martyrdom belong to the same persecution. The former incident might have occurred earlier, but nothing in the sources suggests 203 specifically.

15. See Quentin 1908: 174 for the text. The text gives the name of the proconsul in charge: Rufinus, most often identified as Apuleius Rufinus, consul suffect in 190, who would have succeeded Hilarianus (Birley 1992: 51). Barnes (1985: 266–267, 334;

also 2010: 304–307) suggests that Rufinus should in fact be identified with Minucius Opimianus, which is quite possible. The record of Guden's martyrdom provides no information beyond a rather graphic description of her execution.

16. But not Mavilus of Hadrumetum, if one follows Birley 1991; see above.

17. It must be noted that some scholars do consider the known cases as the "tip of the iceberg," indicative of daily persecution (see, for instance, De Vos 2000: 869–870). However, the only basis for such an hypothesis is the assumption of antagonism between two clearly delineated "Christian" and "pagan" groups in the Greco-Roman cities. The circularity of the argument is obvious.

18. Unfortunately, there is no evidence available for a comparison with other areas, since in most cases the reason for the arrest is not mentioned in the Acts.

19. Nicholson (2009: 68–70) presents as evidence of "communal hostility" the petitions sent in 312 to the emperor Maximin Daia by some cities in Asia Minor. However, Mitchell (1988: 117–119) shows that these "local" petitions are in fact the result of cunning imperial manipulation.

20. See Nicholson 2009 for vocabulary and a balanced analysis, despite a treatment that does not differentiate between the changing contexts of persecution over time from the second to the fourth century.

21. I use the Latin text of Fontaine 1966; translations are mine.

22. I use the Latin text of Azzali Bernardelli 1990b; translations are mine, but see the English translation in Dunn 2004: 107–134.

23. Some scholars tend to assume not only that their ideas had some vitality (Fredouille 1980–81: vol. 1, 24–27) but also that there was a Valentinian "school," if not a teacher, in Carthage at the time of Tertullian (Barnes 1985: 81–82). However, Thomassen (2006: 506) does not find any positive evidence for Valentinians in second- and third-century North Africa. It is true that some Christian groups labeled "Gnostic" (on the category, see Brakke 2010) questioned the value of martyrdom, and on this point the testimony of Tertullian is confirmed both by other heresiologists and by "Gnostic" texts (see Frend 1954; Koschorke 1978: 134–137; Pagels 1980).

24. I use the Latin text of J. J. Thierry, CCSL 2 (1954); my translations are based on that of S. Thelwall, Ante-Nicene Fathers 4 (New York, 1885).

25. On Cyprian and Carthage in the mid-third century, see Sage 1975 and Brent 2010. For Cyprian's letters, I use the Latin text of G. F. Diercks, CCSL 3 (1994–2004), and the English translation, accompanied by a magisterial commentary, by Graeme W. Clarke (1984a, 1984b, 1986, 1989). For the *De lapsis*, I use the text and translation of Maurice Bévenot, Oxford Early Christian Texts (Oxford, 1971).

26. The precise date of the edict is disputed: see Y. Duval 2000; 2005: 175–189.

27. For a thorough discussion and refutation of these positions, see Brent 2010: 123–149.

28. Letter 7 is now unanimously supposed to be the first chronologically in the dossier sent by Cyprian to the Roman clergy in July 250 in order to justify his absence from Carthage (Duquenne 1972: 62–64; Clarke 1984a: 198–199; Deléani 2007: 125–127).

29. Saumagne 1975: 72 ("l'immense majorité"); Sage 1975: 192 ("resistance was weak"; "a great proportion of the community"); Burns 2002: 20 ("a minority seems to have resisted"); Brent 2010: 225 ("a large number").

30. J. Patout Burns seems to follow too closely Cyprian's point of view when he suggests that the dependence of the "community" on the Roman economy weakened its group cohesiveness because the "enforcement of the edict did not affect rich and poor Christians in the same way" (Burns 2002: 15–19, quote at 18).

31. Another type of compromise was to obtain permission from the magistrates to offer only incense in place of an animal sacrifice, and thus become a *turificatus*. Cyprian does not mention any *turificatus* in relation to Carthage but acknowledges that the bishop of Rome, Cornelius, was in communication with some Christians who were in this category (*epist.* 55.2.1).

32. In Letter 7, written when the edict was not yet known (see above), there is no evidence that the strangers are refugees (*epist.* 7.2, with Clarke 1984a: 198; *contra* Brent 2010: 247).

33. For a good narrative, see Sage 1975: 210–266; also Burns 2002.

34. On the persecution of Valerian and Gallienus, see Clarke 2005: 637–647; also Selinger 2002.

35. Latin text in Dolbeau 1983. Musurillo 1972 provides an unreliable Latin text, and caution is required in using his English translation. The historicity of the events that the *Passion* describes is generally accepted.

36. See Barnes 2010: 95: "The riot in Carthage which followed the execution of Cyprian showed the political power of the Christians even at a time of forcible repression." Barnes 2009: 18: by 250 "the Christian church was already a political force which any ... governor of a province where Christians were numerous attempted to oppose at his peril."

37. I cannot offer here a full review of the data, but will in a forthcoming publication.

38. Two cases are attested for North Africa: Maximilian in 295 (see Y. Duval 1995: 33–36; Barnes 2010: 107–108, 379–386) and Marcellus in 298 (Barnes 2010: 108–110).

39. See Löhr 2002 for a refutation of Schwarte's (1994) attempt to prove that there was only one edict.

40. De Ste. Croix defended his positions against Frend's criticisms (Frend 1965a, 1965b: 502–503) in a paper published posthumously (De Ste. Croix 2006: 79–98). See also Shaw 2011: 593, 815.

41. *The Acquittal Proceedings of Felix Bishop of Abthugni* belong to the dossier known as the appendix of Optatus's *Against the Donatists*. I use the Latin text of C. Ziwsa, CSEL 26 (1893), 197–204; English translation in Edwards 1997: 170–180. See Y. Duval 2000: 213–346 for a very detailed reading of the text; also Lepelley 1984 = Lepelley 2001: 321–328.

42. The text mentions some *epistolae salutatoriae*, possibly some liturgical books with readings from Paul's Epistles; see discussion in Y. Duval 2000: 298–303.

43. The expression was borrowed by Henri-Irénée Marrou (Daniélou and Marrou 1963) from the novel *Marius the Epicurian* by Walter Pater (1885).

Chapter 3

1. See Markus 2010: 356–357 on the secular as "an implication of Christian eschatology."

2. Unless otherwise noted, for the works of Augustine I use the Latin text of *Saint Augustine: Opera omnia CAG*, electronic ed., Past Masters (Charlottesville, VA:

InteLex, 2000); English translations are based on that in *The Works of Saint Augustine*, 3rd release, electronic ed., Past Masters (Charlottesville, VA: InteLex, 2011).

3. Dossey (2010: 168–171) tries to determine the audience of anonymous North African sermons from the fourth, fifth, and sixth centuries, among which are a number of Donatist and Arian sermons, but concludes that most of these texts were "utilitarian," "stripped of their original context and shortened."

4. However, see BeDuhn 2010 for a reconstruction of what it was like to be a Manichaean for Augustine.

5. Ann Marie Yasin describes Christians' funerals as "an opportunity for the dramatic outpouring of collective energy and the reinforcement of shared identity among a local community of co-religionists" (2009: 63). However, such a description based on a few literary texts that deal with clergy or ascetics must be contrasted with the picture that emerges from the sermons (Rebillard 2009b: 128–134).

6. Yasin emphasizes how early Christian churches became a space "through which local Christian groups crafted a collective identity" as they came to serve as "venues for the commemoration of the dead through ritualized invocation or through physical memorials" (2009: 47). However, she also carefully notes that "to be buried within the church building at all was already a significant mark of status" (91; see Février 1986: 20).

7. Another very interesting example is that of astrology. Whenever a scriptural passage mentions signs and stars, days and times, Augustine warns his audience not to suppose that they can use this as a justification for their belief in horoscopes. Both the astrologers and their clients were apparently quick to find justification for their beliefs and behavior in scripture. See, for instance, *in euang. Ioh.* 8.8 and 11–12; *serm.* 199.3; and Dolbeau 2003 more generally.

8. See also *serm.* 15A [Denis 21].6. These four sermons were preached in different places and at different times during Augustine's career, so we can assume it was a common theme of his predication.

9. For instance, *serm.* 19.6: "And don't let us expect from the Lord an earthly reward for our good lives. Let us set our sights on the things that are promised to us. Let us place our hearts where they can't go rotten with worldly anxieties. These things which so preoccupy people all pass away, these things all fly off, nothing but a mist is human life on earth (Jas 4:15)." Again, *serm.* 33A [Denis 23].3: "The reason we become Christians is not to have it so good in this life. If that is why we thought we became Christians, to have it good in this temporal life, with a fleeting felicity that evaporates like mist, then we are very gravely mistaken."

10. Latin text in CCSL 149: 30–46.

11. On Augustine's complex attitudes toward this kind of medical practices (on the one hand condemning them as types of magic and on the other providing a loophole to render them acceptable), see Flint 1991: 243–244 and 301–302.

12. On the meaning of *maior*, see Oliveira 2006: 258.

13. Perler 1969: 227. For an attempt at dating the sermon to the year 401, see Hugoniot 1996: 584–588, and 572–590, more generally, for a thorough analysis of the text.

14. On the situation at Simittu, see Hugoniot 1996: 580–584, though he tries a little too hard to extract historical substance from the reported incident.

15. Augustine, *epist.* 117–118; see *PCBE, Afrique*, 279–280, Dioscorus 2; Morgenstern 1993: 79–80.

16. Augustine's Letter 118 contains many references to Dioscorus's life that suggest he was a family friend. It is very likely that his brother is the Zenobius who is the dedicatee of the *De ordine*, a friend of Augustine from his stay in Milan. On Zenobius, see *PCBE, Italie*, Zenobius 1.

17. Augustine, *epist.* 132, 135, and 137. On Rufius Antonius Agrypius Volusianus, see *PLRE* 2: 1184–1185, Volusianus 6; *PCBE, Italie*, 2340–2341, Volusianus 1; Morgenstern 1993: 125. For a thorough analysis of the letters, see Moreau 1973.

18. Albina spent seven years in Africa with her daughter and her husband Pinianus, between 410 and 417, and stayed for a while in Thagaste, where Augustine's good friend Alypius was bishop. See *PCBE, Italie*, 75–77, Albina 2; 1483–1490, Melania 2; Moreau 1973: 53, 123–124.

19. The narrative may not be totally consistent, as Volusianus is said to be "still a Hellene" (Gerontius, *V. Melan.* 50) when Melania decides to visit him in order to save his soul. Though usually interpreted as "pagan," "Hellene" can be a slippery term, as noted by Cameron (2011: 197).

20. Cameron (2011: 197–198) cannot establish that Volusianus was already a catechumen in 411–412; discussion of older arguments in Moreau 1973: 125–126.

21. Augustine, *epist.* 90–91 and 103–104. See *PCBE, Afrique*, 778–779, Nectarius 1; *PLRE* 2: 774, Nectarius 1; Morgenstern 1993: 123–124.

22. Nectarius's religious affiliation has been questioned by O'Donnell (2005: 185–188); see also now Hermanowicz 2008: 166–168 and McLynn 2009: 587. For the traditional view, see Huisman 1956; Lepelley 1979–81: vol. 2, 102; Mandouze and La Bonnardière 1982: 778–779; Morgenstern 1993: 123; Atkins-Dodaro 2001: 242; Bermon 2005.

23. This is the *habitus* identified as typical of late antique elite by Sandwell 2007; see below, note 25.

24. Augustine, *epist.* 152–155. See *PCBE, Afrique*, 659–661, Macedonius 2; *PLRE* 2: 697, Macedonius 3; Morgenstern 1993: 107–108.

25. In her study of John Chrysostom and Libanius in fourth-century Antioch (2007), Isabella Sandwell tends to oppose what I call two hierarchical arrangements of category membership sets. Thus the "habitus" that Chrysostom wanted to reform could be described as an arrangement that gave salience to the religious set in the sole context of private interactions. The evidence I find in contemporary North Africa suggests rather that the conflict was between a hierarchical arrangement and a lateral one.

26. The episode is conventionally dated to 399 with reference to the context of the imperial intervention mentioned above. See, for instance, Morgenstern 1993: 125–126.

27. Gaddis (2005: 118–119) suggests that the destruction of the statue was a gesture of provocation on the part of local circumcellions. However, it is rather difficult to understand why Augustine would have intervened in such a context. Shaw (2011: 249–251) attributes the destruction of the statue to Christian gangsters, in line with his overall interpretation of sectarian violence, but, as he acknowledges, with no evidential support in this particular case.

28. Shaw (2011: 251–259) proposes a very different reading of the Calama episode, mostly, it seems, because he assumes that the *servi Dei* mentioned by Augustine include laypeople. However, in Augustine the phrase *servi Dei*, though it does not have a technical meaning, usually refers to clerics, particularly those living in the episcopal monastery. See Van der Lof 1981; Mandouze 1968: 166 n. 2, 167 n. 5, 204 n. 1, 205 n. 2. Hermanowicz (2004, 2008) does not comment on the term but understands it as designating clerics. Zumkeller reviewed the two hundred occurrences of *servi Dei* in the Augustinian corpus: *epist.* 91.8 is listed among cases for which it is not possible to decide with certainty whether the *servi Dei* are living in a monastery, but they are not in any case laypeople (Zumkeller 1991: 443).

29. The sermons are *serm*. 24 and *serm*. 279 + Morin 1. For the dating in 401, see Perler 1969: 233–234; see Rebillard, forthcoming for the suggestion that the sermon could also be dated to 407. Oliveira 2006 gives a very detailed and informed analysis of the two sermons.

30. The identification holds only if we accept the dating of the sermons to 401.

31. A point well noted in Oliveira 2006: 252.

32. Augustine's choice of Psalm 82 betrays the deliberate intent of rousing his audience's anger, as the few following verses show: "Lord, do not keep silent or hold your peace! Do not be still! Lord! See! Your enemies are in uproar. . . . Fill their face with shame. . . . Let them be humiliated and be downcast forever. Let them perish in disgrace." On chanting verses from the Psalms and the mobilization of the audience, see Shaw 2011: 458–466.

33. Brown 1992: 149–150 on how the Christian church took advantage of this form of political pressure; see Shaw 2011: 441–458 on the importance of shoutings in the life of late antique cities.

34. We may note that Augustine deliberately uses the singular *christianus* when he describes the mutilation: *non egit utique ut a christiano lapis honoraretur, sed ut christianus ille superstitioni ad radendum irasceretur (serm.* 24.6).

35. Oliveira (2006: 259) suggests that the acclamations were shouted the preceding week at the same time as Christians were shouting against the regilding of Hercules' statue, but it cannot be proven.

36. On North Africa, see Rebillard, forthcoming and De Bruyn, forthcoming; for the Greek East, see Fowden 1978.

37. At first glance, this conclusion seems to be contradicted by Brent Shaw's (2011) magisterial study of sectarian violence in late antique North Africa. However, I would like to emphasize that Shaw does not imagine unleashed mobs of Christians attacking pagan statues so much as he attributes the violence to gangs hired or at least encouraged by bishops (see, in particular, 235–243).

Conclusion

1. I paraphrase Brubaker on ethnicity (Brubaker et al. 2006: 363): "In the end, though, our argument is not about how much or how little ethnicity matters; it is about how ethnicity works."

2. Urbach 1959; Baer 1961; Barnes 1985: 97–100.

3. For a strong statement to the contrary, see Boyarin 2009: 11–12.

4. For criticism by Robert Markus, see below. It has been pointed out many times that neither the term "semi-Christian" nor any close equivalent was used in this sense by contemporaries. See, most recently, Soler 2010a, who shows that the term, which is rarely used, designated Christians who Judaized in one way or another, and not former pagans or paganized Christians.

5. See, for instance, Daut (1971), who offers an analysis of Latin sermons from the fourth and fifth centuries, or, more generally, Gemeinhardt 2008: 464–466. Brottier (2004) uses "demi-chrétiens" in a characteristically loose way too; see Brottier 2005.

6. See Sen (2006) for a similar criticism, with what he calls "the presumption of the unique relevance of a singular classification" (11).

7. The secularization of public festivals has been treated extensively by scholars; see Soler 2010b for a critique based on the Antiochian case.

8. This section is also a sort of personal *retractatio*, as I was, along with Claire Sotinel, the principal investigator in a research program on the limits of the secular in late antiquity; see Rebillard and Sotinel 2010.

Bibliography

Adams, Matthew. 2006. "Hybridizing Habitus and Reflexivity: Towards an Understanding of Contemporary Identity?" *Sociology* 40 (3): 511–528.
Alikin, Valeriy A. 2010. *The Earliest History of the Christian Gathering: Origin, Development, and Content of the Christian Gathering in the First to Third Centuries*. Supplements to Vigiliae Christianae 102. Leiden: Brill.
Altman, Janet Gurkin. 1982. *Epistolarity: Approaches to a Form*. Columbus: Ohio State University Press.
Amat, Jacqueline, ed., trans., and annot. 1996. *Passion de Perpétue et de Félicité; suivi des Actes*. Sources Chrétiennes 417. Paris: Éditions du Cerf.
———. 1998. "Les persécutions contre les chrétiens et l'hostilité populaire, dans la première moitié du IIIe siècle en Afrique." *Euphrosyne* 26: 293–300.
Asad, Talal. 1993. *Genealogies of Religion: Discipline and Reasons of Power in Christianity and Islam*. Baltimore: Johns Hopkins University Press.
Atkins, E. Margaret, and Robert Dodaro. 2001. *Augustine: Political Writings*. Cambridge Texts in the History of Political Thought. Cambridge: Cambridge University Press.
Aviam, Mordechai. 2004. *Jews, Pagans, and Christians in the Galilee: 25 Years of Archaeological Excavations and Surveys; Hellenistic to Byzantine Periods*. Land of Galilee 1. Rochester, NY: University of Rochester Press.
Aziza, Claude. 1974. "Recherches sur l'onokoitès des écrits apologétiques de Tertullien." *Annales de la faculté des lettres et sciences humaines de Nice* 21: 283–290.
Azzali Bernardelli, Giovanna. 1990a. "*De quaestionibus confessionum alibi docebimus* (Tertulliano, *Cor.* 1, 5)." In *Hommage à René Braun*, vol. 2, *Autour de Tertullien*, edited by Jean Granarolo and Michèle Biraud, 51–84. Paris: Les Belles Lettres.
———. ed., trans., and annot. 1990b. *Tertulliano, Scorpiace*. Biblioteca Patristica 14. Florence: Nardini.
Baer, Yitzhak. 1961. "Israel, the Christian Church, and the Roman Empire from the Time of Septimius Severus to the Edict of Toleration of AD 313." *Scripta Hierosolymitana* 73: 79–149.
Barnes, Timothy David. 1968. "Legislation against the Christians." *Journal of Roman Studies* 58 (1–2): 32–50.
———. 1969. "Tertullian's *Scorpiace*." *Journal of Theological Studies* 20: 105–132.
———. 1971. "Three Neglected Martyrs." *Journal of Theological Studies* 22: 159–161.
———. 1985. *Tertullian: A Historical and Literary Study*. Rev. ed. Oxford: Oxford University Press.
———. 2009. "Aspects of Severan Empire II: Christians in Roman Provincial Society." *New England Classical Journal* 36: 3–19.

———. 2010. *Early Christian Hagiography and Roman History.* Tria Corda 5. Tübingen: Mohr Siebeck.
Bastiaensen, Antoon A. R., ed., trans., and annot. 1975. *Atti e passioni dei martiri.* Scrittori Greci e Latini. Milan: A. Mondadori; Fondazione Lorenzo Valla.
Baxter, J. H. 1924. "The Martyrs of Madaura a.d. 180." *Journal of Theological Studies* 26: 31–37.
Beard, Mary, John A. North, and Simon R. F. Price. 1998. *Religions of Rome.* 2 vols. Cambridge: Cambridge University Press.
BeDuhn, Jason. 2000. *The Manichaean Body: In Discipline and Ritual.* Baltimore: Johns Hopkins University Press.
———. 2010. *Augustine's Manichaean Dilemma: 1, Conversion and Apostasy, 373–388 C.E.* Divinations: Rereading Ancient Religion. Philadelphia: University of Pennsylvania Press.
Bendlin, Andreas. 2000. "Looking beyond the Civic Compromise: Religious Pluralism in Late Republican Rome." In *Religion in Archaic and Republican Rome and Italy: Evidence and Experience*, edited by Edward Bispham and Christopher Smith, 115–135. Edinburgh: Edinburgh University Press.
Benko, Stephen. 1980. "Pagan Criticism of Christianity during the First Two Centuries." In *Aufstieg und Niedergang der Römischen Welt*, II, 23.2, edited by Hildegard Temporini and Wolfgang Haase, 1054–1118. Berlin: De Gruyter.
Benseddik, Nacéra. 1989. "La pratique médicinale en Afrique au temps d'Augustin." In *L'Africa Romana, 2, Atti del VI Convegno di studio*, 663–682. Sassari: Edizioni Gallizzi.
Berardino, Angelo di. 1972. "Maestri cristiani del III secolo nell'insegnamento classico." *Augustinianum* 12 (3): 549–556.
Bermon, Emmanuel. 2005. "Nectarius." In *Dictionnaire des philosophes antiques,* vol. 4, *De Labeo à Ovidius*, edited by Richard Goulet, 615–617. Paris: Éditions du Centre National de la Recherche Scientifique.
Birley, Anthony R. 1991. "A Persecuting Praeses of Numidia under Valerian." *Journal of Theological Studies* 42: 598–610.
———. 1992. "Persecutors and Martyrs in Tertullian's Africa." *Bulletin of the Institute of Archaeology of the University of London* 29: 37–68.
———. 2005. *The Roman Government of Britain.* Oxford: Oxford University Press.
Bobertz, Charles Arnold. 1988. "Cyprian of Carthage as Patron: A Social Historical Study of the Role of Bishop in the Ancient Christian Community of North Africa." PhD diss., Yale University.
Bonner, Gerald. 1984. "The Extinction of Paganism and the Church Historian." *Journal of Ecclesiastical History* 35: 339–357.
Bourdieu, Pierre. 1977. *Outline of a Theory of Practice.* Cambridge Studies in Social Anthropology 16. Cambridge: Cambridge University Press.
———. 1990. *The Logic of Practice.* Stanford, CA: Stanford University Press.
———. 2000. *Pascalian Meditations.* Stanford, CA: Stanford University Press.
Bowersock, G. W. 1995. *Martyrdom and Rome.* The Wiles Lectures. Cambridge: Cambridge University Press.
Boyarin, Daniel. 2009. "Rethinking Jewish Christianity: An Argument for Dismantling a Dubious Category (to Which Is Appended a Correction of My *Border Lines*)." *Jewish Quarterly Review* 99 (1): 7–36.

Brakke, David. 2010. *The Gnostics: Myth, Ritual, and Diversity in Early Christianity.* Cambridge, MA: Harvard University Press.

Brandenburg, Hugo. 1994. "Coemeterium: Der Wandel des Bestattungswesens als Zeichen des Kulturumbrucks der Spätantike." *Laverna* 5: 206–232.

Braun, René. 1966. "Le problème des deux livres du *De cultu feminarum* de Tertullien: Un ouvrage homogène ou deux écrits distincts?" In *Studia Patristica*, vol. 7, *Papers Presented to the Fourth International Conference on Patristic Studies Held at Christ Church, Oxford, 1963*, edited by F. L. Cross, 133–142. Berlin: Akademie-Verlag.

———. 1972. "Un nouveau Tertullien: Problèmes de biographie et de chronologie." *Revue des études latines* 50: 67–84.

———. 1977. *Deus Christianorum: Recherches sur le vocabulaire doctrinal de Tertullien.* 2nd ed., rev. and augm. Paris: Études Augustiniennes.

———. 1978. "Sur la date, la composition et le texte de l'*Ad Martyras* de Tertullien." *Revue des études augustiniennes* 24: 221–242.

Brennan, C. 2008. "Tertullian's *De Pallio* and Roman Dress in North Africa." In *Roman Dress and the Fabrics of Roman Culture.* Phoenix supp. vol. 46, edited by Jonathan C. Edmondson and Alison Keith, 257–270. Toronto: University of Toronto Press.

Brent, Allen. 1995. *Hippolytus and the Roman Church in the Third Century: Communities in Tension before the Emergence of a Monarch-Bishop.* Supplements to Vigiliae Christianae 31. Leiden: Brill.

———. 2010. *Cyprian and Roman Carthage.* Cambridge: Cambridge University Press.

Brottier, Laurence. 2004. "Jean Chrysostome: Un pasteur face à des 'demi-chrétiens'." In *Antioche de Syrie: Histoire, images et traces de la ville antique*, edited by Bernadette Cabouret, Pierre-Louis Gatier, and Catherine Saliou, 439–457. Lyon: Maison de l'Orient Méditerranéen.

———. 2005. *L'appel des 'demi-chrétiens' à la 'vie angélique': Jean Chrysostome prédicateur; Entre idéal monastique et réalité mondaine.* Paris: Éditions du Cerf.

Brown, Peter R. L. 1961. "Aspects of the Christianization of the Roman Aristocracy." *Journal of Roman Studies* 51: 1–11.

———. 1992. *Power and Persuasion in Late Antiquity: Towards a Christian Empire.* Madison: University of Wisconsin Press.

———. 1995. *Authority and the Sacred: Aspects of the Christianisation of the Roman World.* Cambridge: Cambridge University Press.

———. 1998. "Christianization and Religious Conflict." In *The Cambridge Ancient History,* vol. 13, *The Late Empire, A.D. 337–425,* edited by Averil Cameron and Peter Garnsey, 632–664. Cambridge: Cambridge University Press.

Brubaker, Rogers. 2002. "Ethnicity without Groups." *Archives européennes de sociologie* 43 (2): 163–189.

———. 2004. *Ethnicity without Groups.* Cambridge, MA: Harvard University Press.

Brubaker, Rogers, and Frederick Cooper. 2000. "Beyond 'Identity'." *Theory and Society* 29 (1): 1–47.

Brubaker, Rogers, Margit Feischmidt, Jon Fox, and Liana Grancea. 2006. *Nationalist Politics and Everyday Ethnicity in a Transylvanian Town.* Princeton, NJ: Princeton University Press.

Bruyn, Gabriel de. Forthcoming. "*Os habent et non loquentur.* La mutilation des statues divines en Afrique dans l'antiquité tardive." In *Faire parler et faire taire les statues*, edited by Yann Rivière. Rome: École Française de Rome.

Burke, Peter J. 2003. "Relationships between Multiple Identities." In *Advances in Identity Theory and Research*, edited by Peter J. Burke, Timothy J. Owens, Richard Serpe, and Peggy A. Thoits, 195–214. New York: Kluwer Academic/Plenum Publishers.

Burke, Peter J., and Jan E. Stets. 2009. *Identity Theory*. Oxford: Oxford University Press.

Burns, J. Patout. 2002. *Cyprian the Bishop*. Routledge Early Church Monographs. London: Routledge.

Calef, Susan A. 1996. "Rhetorical Strategies in Tertullian's *De Cultu Feminarum*." PhD diss., University of Notre Dame.

Cameron, Alan. 2011. *The Last Pagans of Rome*. New York: Oxford University Press.

Carletti, Carlo. 2008. *Epigrafia dei cristiani in Occidente dal III al VII secolo: Ideologia e prassi*. Inscriptiones Christianae Italiae. Subsidia 6. Bari: Edipuglia.

Casiday, Augustine, and Frederick W. Norris, eds. 2007. *The Cambridge History of Christianity*. Vol. 2, *Constantine to c. 600*. Cambridge: Cambridge University Press.

Chadwick, Henry. 1985. "Augustine on Pagans and Christians: Reflections on Religious and Social Change." In *History, Society, and the Churches: Essays in Honour of Owen Chadwick*, edited by Derek Beales and Geoffrey Best, 9–27. Cambridge: Cambridge University Press.

Chastagnol, André. 1956. "Le sénateur Volusien et la conversion d'une famille de l'aristocratie romaine au Bas Empire." *Revue des études anciennes* 58: 241–253.

Choat, Malcolm. 2006. *Belief and Cult in Fourth-Century Papyri*. Studia Antiqua Australiensia 1. Turnhout: Brepols.

Christian, William A. 1981. *Local Religion in Sixteenth-Century Spain*. Princeton, NJ: Princeton University Press.

Clark, Elizabeth A. 1998. "Holy Women, Holy Words: Early Christian Woman, Social History, and the 'Linguistic Turn'." *Journal of Early Christian Studies* 6 (3): 413–430.

———. 2004. *History, Theory, Text: Historians and the Linguistic Turn*. Cambridge, MA: Harvard University Press.

Clarke, Graeme W. 1969. "Some Observations on the Persecution of Decius." *Antichton* 3: 63–76.

———. 1973a. "Double-Trials in the Persecution of Decius." *Historia* 22: 650–663.

———. 1973b. "Two Measures in the Persecution of Decius? Two Recent Views." *Bulletin of the Institute of Classical Studies of the University of London* 20: 118–123.

———, trans. and annot. 1974. *The Octavius of Marcus Minucius Felix*. Ancient Christian Writers 39. New York: Newman Press.

———, trans. and annot. 1984a. *The Letters of St. Cyprian of Carthage*. Vol. 1, *Letters 1–27*. Ancient Christian Writers 43. New York: Newman Press.

———, trans. and annot. 1984b. *The Letters of St. Cyprian of Carthage*. Vol. 2, *Letters 28–54*. Ancient Christian Writers 44. New York: Newman Press.

———, trans. and annot. 1986. *The Letters of St. Cyprian of Carthage*. Vol. 3, *Letters 55–66*. Ancient Christian Writers 46. New York: Newman Press.

———, trans. and annot. 1989. *The Letters of St. Cyprian of Carthage*. Vol. 4, *Letters 67–82*. Ancient Christian Writers 47. New York: Newman Press.

———. 2005. "Third-Century Christianity." In *The Cambridge Ancient History*, vol. 12, *The Crisis of Empire, A.D. 193–337*, edited by Alan K. Bowman, Peter Garnsey, and Averil Cameron, 589–671. Cambridge: Cambridge University Press.
Cohen, Shaye J. D. 1999. *The Beginnings of Jewishness: Boundaries, Varieties, Uncertainties*. Hellenistic Culture and Society 31. Berkeley: University of California Press.
Cooper, Kate. 2011. "A Father, a Daughter and a Procurator: Authority and Resistance in the Prison Memoir of Perpetua of Carthage." *Gender & History* 23 (3): 685–702.
Courcelle, Pierre. 1964. *Histoire littéraire des grandes invasions germaniques*. 3rd ed. Paris: Études augustiniennes.
Daguet-Gagey, Anne. 2001. "Septime Sévère, un empereur persécuteur des chrétiens?" *Revue des études augustiniennes* 47: 3–32.
Daniélou, Jean, and Henri-Irénée Marrou. 1963. *Nouvelle histoire de l'Église*. Vol. 1, *Des origines à Saint Grégoire le Grand*. Paris: Éditions du Seuil.
Daut, Winfried. 1971. "Die 'halben Christen' unter den konvertiten und gebildeten des 4. und 5. Jahrhunderts." *Zeitschrift für Missionswissenschaft und Religionswissenschaft* 55: 171–188.
Deferrari, Roy J. 1922. "St. Augustine's Method of Composing and Delivering Sermons." *American Journal of Philology* 43: 97–123, 193–219.
Deléani, Simone, trans. and annot. 2007. *Saint Cyprien: Lettres 1–20*. Collection des Études Augustiniennes. Série Antiquité 182. Paris: Institut d'Études Augustiniennes.
De Ste. Croix, Geoffrey E. M. 1954. "Aspects of the Great Persecution." *Harvard Theological Review* 47: 75–113.
———. 1963. "Why Were the Early Christians Persecuted?" *Past and Present* 26: 6–38.
———. 2006. *Christian Persecution, Martyrdom, and Orthodoxy*. Edited by Michael Whitby and Joseph Streeter. Oxford: Oxford University Press.
De Vos, Craig. 2000. "Popular Graeco-Roman Responses to Christianity." In *The Early Christian World*, edited by Philip F. Esler, 2: 869–889. London: Routledge.
Dietz, Karlheinz. 1997. "Iulius Asper, Verteidiger der Provinzen unter Septimius Severus." *Chiron* 27: 483–523.
Dolbeau, François. 1983. "La Passion des saints Lucius et Montanus: Histoire et édition du texte." *Revue des études augustiniennes* 29: 39–82.
———. 1993. "Nouveaux sermons de saint Augustin pour la conversion des païens et des donatistes (VI)." *Revue des études augustiniennes* 39: 371–423.
———. 1996. *Vingt-six sermons au peuple d'Afrique*. Collection des Études Augustiniennes. Série Antiquité 147. Paris: Institut d'Études Augustiniennes.
———. 1998. "La survie des œuvres d'Augustin: Remarques sur l'Indiculum attribué à Possidius et sur la bibliothèque d'Anségise." In *Du copiste au collectionneur: Mélanges d'histoire des textes et des bibliothèques en l'honneur d'André Vernet*, edited by Donatella Nebbiai-Dalla Guarda, Jean François Genest and André Vernet, 3–22. Bibliologia 18. Turnhout: Brepols.
———. 2003. "Le combat pastoral d'Augustin contre les astrologues, les devins et les guérisseurs." In *Augustinus Afer: Saint Augustin: africanité et universalité: Actes du colloque international, Alger-Annaba, 1–7 avril 2001*, edited by Pierre-Yves Fux, Jean-Michel Roessli, and Otto Wermelinger, 1: 167–182. Paradosis 45. Fribourg: Éditions universitaires.

Dölger, Franz Joseph. 1958. "Beitrage zur Geschichte des Kreuzzeichens I." *Jahrbuch für Antike und Christentum* 1: 5–13.

Dossey, Leslie. 2010. *Peasant and Empire in Christian North Africa*. The Transformation of the Classical Heritage 47. Berkeley: University of California Press.

Drinkwater, John. 2005. "Maximinus to Diocletian and the 'Crisis'." In *The Cambridge Ancient History*, vol. 12, *The Crisis of Empire, A.D. 193–337*, edited by Alan K. Bowman, Peter Garnsey, and Averil Cameron, 28–66. Cambridge: Cambridge University Press.

Ducloux, Anne. 1994. *Ad ecclesiam confugere: Naissance du droit d'asile dans les églises (IVe-milieu du Ve s.)*. De l'Archéologie à l'Histoire. Paris: De Boccard.

Dunn, Geoffrey D. 2004. *Tertullian*. The Early Church Fathers. London: Routledge.

———. 2005. "Mavilus of Hadrumetum, African Proconsuls and Mediaeval Martyrologies." In *Studies in Latin Literature and Roman History XII*, edited by Carl Deroux, 433–446. Collection Latomus 287. Brussels: Éditions Latomus.

Duquenne, Luc. 1972. *Chronologie des lettres de s. Cyprien: Le dossier de la persécution de Dèce*. Subsidia Hagiographica 54. Brussels: Société des Bollandistes.

Duval, Noël. 1977. "Observations sur l'onomastique dans les inscriptions chrétiennes d'Afrique du Nord." In *L'onomastique latine: Actes du Colloque international sur l'onomastique latine, Paris, 13–15 Octobre 1975*, edited by Noël Duval, 447–456. Paris: Centre National de la Recherche Scientifique.

———. 1988. "L'épigraphie funéraire chrétienne d'Afrique: Traditions et ruptures, constantes et diversités." In *La terza età dell'epigrafia: Colloque AIEGL-Borghèse 86, Bologna, Ottobre 1986*, edited by Angela Donati, 265–314. Faenza: Fratelli Lega.

Duval, Yvette. 1982. *Loca sanctorum Africae: Le culte des martyrs en Afrique du IVe au VIIe siècle*. 2 vols. Collection de l'École Française de Rome 58. Rome: École Française de Rome.

———. 1995. *Lambèse chrétienne, la gloire et l'oubli: De la Numidie romaine à l'Ifrîqiya*. Collection des Études Augustiniennes. Série Antiquité 144. Paris: Institut des Études Augustiniennes.

———. 2000. *Chrétiens d'Afrique à l'aube de la paix constantinienne: Les premiers échos de la grande persécution*. Collection des Études Augustiniennes. Série Antiquité 164. Paris: Institut d'Études Augustiniennes.

———. 2001. "Celerinus et les siens d'après la correspondance de Cyprien: (*Ep.* 21–23, 37, 39)." *Revue des études augustiniennes* 47 (1): 33–62.

———. 2005. *Les chrétientés d'Occident et leur évêque au IIIe siècle: Plebs in ecclesia constitua (Cyprien, Ep. 63)*. Collection des Études Augustiniennes. Série Antiquité 176. Paris: Institut d'Études Augustiniennes.

Ebbeler, Jennifer V. 2001. "Pedants in the Apparel of Heroes? Cultures of Latin Letter-Writing from Cicero to Ennodius." PhD diss., University of Pennsylvania.

Edwards, Douglas R. 1996. *Religion and Power: Pagans, Jews, and Christians in the Greek East*. New York: Oxford University Press.

Edwards, Mark J., trans. 1997. *Optatus: Against the Donatists*. Translated Texts for Historians 27. Liverpool: Liverpool University Press.

———. 2004. "Dating Arnobius: Why Discount the Evidence of Jerome?" *Antiquité tardive* 12: 263–271.

Edwards, Mark J., Martin Goodman, Simon Price, and Christopher Rowland, eds. 1999. *Apologetics in the Roman Empire: Pagans, Jews, and Christians.* Oxford: Oxford University Press.

Engberg, Jakob. 2007. *Impulsore Chresto: Opposition to Christianity in the Roman Empire, c. 50–250 AD.* Early Christianity in the Context of Antiquity 2. Frankfurt am Main: Peter Lang.

Errington, Robert Malcolm. 1997. "Christian Accounts of the Religious Legislation of Theodosius I." *Klio* 79 (2): 398–443.

———. 2006. *Roman Imperial Policy from Julian to Theodosius.* Studies in the History of Greece and Rome. Chapel Hill: University of North Carolina Press.

Fishwick, Duncan. 1984. "Pliny and the Christians: The Rites *Ad imaginem principis*." *American Journal of Ancient History* 9: 123–127.

Flint, Valerie I. J. 1991. *The Rise of Magic in Early Medieval Europe.* Princeton, NJ: Princeton University Press.

Fontaine, Jacques, ed. and annot. 1966. *Tertullien, Sur la Couronne.* Collection Érasme 18. Paris: Presses Universitaires de France.

Fowden, Garth. 1978. "Bishops and Temples in the Eastern Roman Empire A.D. 320–435." *Journal of Theological Studies* 29 (1): 53–78.

Fox, Jon E., and Cynthia Miller-Idriss. 2008. "Everyday Nationhood." *Ethnicities* 8 (4): 536–563.

Franchi de' Cavalieri, Pio. 1909. "Nuove osservazione critiche ed esegetiche sul testo della *Passio Sanctorum Montani et Lucii*." In Pio Franchi de' Cavalieri, *Note Agiografiche,* 3: 3–114. Studi e Testi 22. Rome: Tip. Vaticana.

Frankfurter, David. 2002. "Dynamics of Ritual Expertise in Antiquity and Beyond: Towards a New Taxonomy of 'Magicians'." In *Magic and Ritual in the Ancient World,* edited by Paul Mirecki and Marvin Meyer, 159–178. Leiden: Brill.

———. 2005. "Beyond Magic and Superstition." In *A People's History of Christianity,* vol. 2, *Late Ancient Christianity,* edited by Virginia Burrus, 255–284. Minneapolis: Fortress Press.

Fredouille, Jean-Claude, ed., trans., and annot. 1980–81. *Tertullien, Contre les Valentiniens.* 2 vols. Sources Chrétiennes 280–281. Paris: Éditions du Cerf.

Frend, William H. C. 1954. "The Gnostic Sects and the Roman Empire." *Journal of Ecclesiastical History* 5: 25–37.

———. 1965a. "A Note on the Great Persecution in the West." In *Papers read at the second winter and summer meetings of the Ecclesiastical History Society,* 141–148. Studies in Church History 2. London: Nelson.

———. 1965b. *Martyrdom and Persecution in the Early Church.* Oxford: Blackwell.

———. 1985. *The Donatist Church: A Movement of Protest in Roman North Africa.* Third Impression. Oxford: Clarendon Press.

Freudenberger, R. 1970. "Der Anlass zu Tertullians Schrift *De Corona Militis*." *Historia* 19: 579–592.

Gaddis, Michael. 2005. *There Is No Crime for Those Who Have Christ: Religious Violence in the Christian Roman Empire.* Transformation of the Classical Heritage 39. Berkeley: University of California Press.

Gemeinhardt, Peter. 2008. "Staatsreligion, Volkskirche oder Gemeinschaft der Heiligen? Das Christentum in der Spätantike: eine Standortbestimmung." *Zeitschrift für Antikes Christentum* 3: 453–476.

Giddens, Anthony. 1991. *Modernity and Self-Identity: Self and Society in the Late Modern Age*. Stanford, CA: Stanford University Press.

Giovannini, Adalberto. 1984. "Tacite, l'*incendium Neronis* et les chrétiens." *Revue des études augustiniennes* 30 (1): 3–23.

———. 1996. "L'interdit contre les chrétiens: Raison d'état ou mesure de police?" *Cahiers du Centre Gustave-Glotz* 7: 103–134.

Grattarola, Pio. 1984. "Il problema dei lapsi fra Roma e Carthagine." *Rivista di storia della chiesa in Italia* 38: 1–26.

Gregg, Robert C., and Dan Urman, eds. 1996. *Jews, Pagans, and Christians in the Golan Heights: Greek and Other Inscriptions of the Roman and Byzantine Eras*. South Florida Studies in the History of Judaism 140. Atlanta: Scholars Press.

Grig, Lucy. 2004. *Making Martyrs in Late Antiquity*. London: Duckworth.

Groh, Dennis E. 1971. "Tertullian's Polemic against Social Co-Optation." *Church History* 40: 7–14.

———. 1976. "Upper-Class Christians in Tertullian's Africa: Some Observations." In *Studia Patristica*, vol. 14, *Papers Presented to the Sixth International Conference on Patristic Studies Held in Oxford, 1971*, edited by Elizabeth A. Livingstone, 41–47. Berlin: Akademie-Verlag.

Gros, Pierre. 2000. "Carthage romaine: Résurrection d'une capitale." In *Mégapoles méditerranéennes: Géographie urbaine rétrospective*, edited by Jean-Charles Depaule, Robert Ilbert, and Claude Nicolet, 534–544. Collection de l'École Française de Rome 261. Rome: École Française de Rome, 2000.

Guignebert, Charles. 1923. "Les demi-chrétiens et leur place dans l'Église antique." *Revue de l'histoire des religions* 88: 65–102.

Handelman, Don. 1977. "The Organization of Ethnicity." *Ethnic Groups* 1: 187–200.

Harland, Philip A. 2003. *Associations, Synagogues, and Congregations: Claiming a Place in Ancient Mediterranean Society*. Minneapolis: Fortress Press.

———. 2009. *Dynamics of Identity in the World of the Early Christians: Associations, Judeans, and Cultural Minorities*. New York: T & T Clark.

Harmless, William. 1995. *Augustine and the Catechumenate*. Collegeville, MN: Liturgical Press.

———. 2004. "The Voice and the Word: Augustine's Catechumenate in Light of the Dolbeau Sermons." *Augustinian Studies* 35 (1): 17–42.

Helgeland, John. 1979. "Christians and the Roman Army from Marcus Aurelius to Constantine." In *Aufstieg und Niedergang der Römischen Welt*, II, 23.1, edited by Hildegard Temporini and Wolfgang Haase, 724–834. Berlin: De Gruyter.

Hermanowicz, Erika. 2004. "Catholic Bishops and Appeals to the Imperial Court: A Legal Study of the Calama Riots in 408." *Journal of Early Christian Studies* 12 (4): 481–521.

———. 2008. *Possidius of Calama: A Study of the North African Episcopate at the Time of Augustine*. Oxford Early Christian Studies. Oxford: Clarendon Press.

Hobsbawm, Eric J. 1990. *Nations and Nationalism since 1780: Programme, Myth, Reality*. Cambridge: Cambridge University Press.

Hopkins, Keith. 1998. "Christian Number and Its Implications." *Journal of Early Christian Studies* 6 (2): 185–226.

———. 1999. *A World Full of Gods: Pagans, Jews, and Christians in the Roman Empire*. London: Weidenfeld & Nicolson.

Horsley, Greg H. R. 1987. "Name Change as an Indication of Religious Conversion in Antiquity." *Numen* 34: 1–17.

Hugoniot, Christophe. 1996. "Les spectacles de l'Afrique Romaine: Une culture officielle municipale sous l'empire romain." PhD diss., Université de Paris 4-Sorbonne.

Huisman, H., trans. and annot. 1956. *Augustinus' Briefwisseling met Nectarius: Inleiding, Tekst, Vertalung, Commentar.* Amsterdam: J. Babeliowsky.

Hunter, David G. 2003. "Augustine and the Making of Marriage in Roman North Africa." *Journal of Early Christian Studies* 11 (1): 63–85.

James, William. 1890. *The Principles of Psychology.* New York: H. Holt and Company.

Janowitz, Naomi. 2001. *Magic in the Roman World: Pagans, Jews, and Christians.* London: Routledge.

Kahlos, Maijastina. 2004. "*Incerti* in between: Moments of Transition and Dialogue in Christian Polemics in the Fourth and Fifth Centuries." *Parola del passato* 59 (334): 5–24.

———. 2007. *Debate and Dialogue: Christian and Pagan Cultures, c. 360–430.* Ashgate New Critical Thinking in Religion, Theology, and Biblical Studies. Aldershot, UK: Ashgate.

Kajanto, Iiro. 1963. *Onomastic Studies in the Early Christian Inscriptions of Rome and Carthage.* Acta Instituti Romani Finlandiae 2/1. Helsinki: Institutum Romanum Finlandiae.

Keresztes, Paul. 1989. *Imperial Rome and the Christians.* 2 vols. Lanham, MD: University Press of America.

Koschorke, Klaus. 1978. *Die Polemik der Gnostiker gegen das Kirchliche Christentum: Unter besonderer Berücksichtigung der Nag-Hammadi-Traktate 'Apokalypse des Petrus' (NHC VII,3) und 'Testimonium Veritatis' (NHC IX,3).* Nag Hammadi Studies 12. Leiden: Brill.

Kraemer, Ross Shepard. 1992. *Her Share of the Blessings: Women's Religions among Pagans, Jews, and Christians in the Greco-Roman World.* New York: Oxford University Press.

Kraemer, Ross Shepard, and Shira L. Lander. 2000. "Perpetua and Felicitas." In *The Early Christian World*, edited by Philip F. Esler, 2: 1048–1068. London: Routledge.

Labriolle, Pierre Champagne de. 1934. *La réaction païenne: Étude sur la polémique antichrétienne du Ier au VIe siècle.* Paris: L'Artisan du Livre.

LaCapra, Dominick. 1985. *History & Criticism.* Ithaca, NY: Cornell University Press.

Lahire, Bernard. 2003. "From the Habitus to an Individual Heritage of Dispositions: Towards a Sociology at the Level of the Individual." *Poetics* 31 (5–6): 329–355.

———. 2004. *La culture des individus: Dissonances culturelles et distinction de soi.* Paris: La Découverte.

———. 2011. *The Plural Actor.* Translated by David Fernbach. Cambridge: Polity.

Lamirande, Emilien. 1992. "Catechumenus." In *Augustinus-Lexikon,* 1, 5–6, edited by Cornelius Mayer, 788–794. Basel: Schwabe.

Lanata, Giuliana. 1973. *Gli atti dei martiri come documenti processuali.* Studi e Testi per un Corpus Iudicorum 1. Milan: Giuffrè.

Lancel, Serge. 1964. "Monsieur Dupont, en Latin." In *Hommages à Jean Bayet*, 357–364. Brussels: Editions Latomus.

———. 1999. "Le Proconsul Anullinus et la grande persécution en Afrique en 303–304 ap. J.-C.: Nouveaux documents." *Comptes rendus de l'Académie des Inscriptions et Belles Lettres* 1999 (3): 1013–1022.

———. 2002. *Saint Augustine*. Translated by Antonia Nevill. London: SCM Press.

Lane Fox, Robin. 1987. *Pagans and Christians*. New York: Knopf.

Lassère, Jean Marie. 1977. *Ubique populus: Peuplement et mouvements de population dans l'Afrique romaine de la chute de Carthage à la fin de la dynastie des Sévères (146 a.C.–235 p.C.)*. Etudes d'Antiquités Africaines. Paris: Éditions du Centre National de la Recherche Scientifique.

Le Bohec, Yann. 1992. "Tertullien, *De Corona*, 1: Carthage ou Lambèse?" *Revue des études augustiniennes* 38: 6–18.

Lepelley, Claude. 1979–81. *Les cités de l'Afrique romaine au Bas-Empire*. 2 vols. Collection des Études Augustiniennes. Paris: Études Augustiniennes.

———. 1984. "Chrétiens et païens au temps de la persécution de Dioclétien: Le cas d'Abthugnî." In *Studia Patristica*, vol. 15, *Papers Presented to the VIth Conference of Patristic Studies, Oxford, 1975*, 226–232. Berlin: Akademie-Verlag. Reprinted in Claude Lepelley, *Aspects de l'Afrique romaine: Les cités, la vie rurale, le christianisme*, Munera 15 (Bari: Edipuglia, 2001), 321–328.

———. 1987. "Spes saeculi: Le milieu social d'Augustin et ses ambitions séculières avant sa conversion." In *Congresso internazionale su S. Agostino nel XVI centenario della conversione, Roma 15–20 Settembre 1986*, 99–117. Rome: Institutum Patristicum "Augustinianum."

———. 1992. "Circumcelliones." In *Augustinus-Lexikon*, 1, 5–6, edited by Cornelius Mayer, 930–936. Basel: Schwabe.

———. 1994. "Le musée des statues divines: La volonté de sauvegarder le patrimoine artistique païen à l'époque théodosienne." *Cahiers archéologiques* 42: 5–15.

———. 1999. "L'apport d'actes des martyrs nouvellement découverts à la connaissance de la géographie historique de l'Afrique Proconsulaire." *Bulletin de la Société nationale des antiquaires de France*: 205–221.

———. 2001. *Aspects de l'Afrique romaine: Les cités, la vie rurale, le christianisme*. Munera 15. Bari: Edipuglia.

———. 2002. "Le lieu des valeurs communes: La cité terrain neutre entre païens et chrétiens dans l'Afrique romaine tardive." In *Idéologies et valeurs civiques dans le monde romain: Hommage à Claude Lepelley*, edited by Hervé Inglebert, 271–285. Paris: Picard.

Leroy, François-Joseph. 1999. "Les 22 inédits de la catéchèse donatiste de Vienne: Une édition provisoire." *Recherches augustiniennes* 31: 149–234.

Lieu, Judith. 2004. *Christian Identity in the Jewish and Graeco-Roman World*. Oxford: Oxford University Press.

Lieu, Judith, John North, and Tessa Rajak, eds. 1992. *The Jews among Pagans and Christians: In the Roman Empire*. London: Routledge.

Lo Cascio, Elio. 2003. "Una possibile testimonianza sul valore dell'*antoninianus* negli anni di Decio?" In *Consuetudinis Amor: Fragments d'histoire romaine (IIe-VIe siècles) offerts à Jean-Pierre Callu*, edited by François Chausson and Étienne Wolff, 299–309. Rome: L'Erma di Bretschneider.

Löhr, Winrich A. 2002. "Some Observations on Karl-Heinz Schwarte's Diocletian's Christengesetz." *Vigiliae Christianae* 56 (1): 75–95.

Lomanto, Valeria. 1975. "Rapporti fra la *Passio Perpetuae* e *Passiones* africane." In *Forma Futuri: Studi in onore del cardinale Michele Pellegrino*, 566–586. Turin: Bottega d'Erasmo.

MacCormack, Sabine. 1998. *The Shadows of Poetry: Vergil in the Mind of Augustine*. Transformation of the Classical Heritage 26. Berkeley: University of California Press.

MacMullen, Ramsay. 1981. *Paganism in the Roman Empire*. New Haven, CT: Yale University Press.

———. 1984. *Christianizing the Roman Empire (A.D. 100–400)*. New Haven, CT: Yale University Press.

———. 1989. "The Preacher's Audience." *Journal of Theological Studies* 40: 503–511.

———. 1997. *Christianity and Paganism in the Fourth to Eighth Centuries*. New Haven, CT: Yale University Press.

———. 2009. *The Second Church: Popular Christianity, A.D. 200–400*. Society of Biblical Literature Writings from the Greco-Roman World Supplement Series 1. Atlanta: Society of Biblical Literature.

Madec, Goulven. 1992. "Le Christ des païens d'après le *De consensu evangelistarum* de saint Augustin." *Recherches augustiniennes* 26: 3–67.

Maier, Jean Louis. 1973. *L'épiscopat de l'Afrique romaine, vandale, et byzantine*. Bibliotheca Helvetica Romana 11. Rome: Institut Suisse de Rome.

Mandouze, André. 1968. *Saint Augustin, l'aventure de la raison et de la grâce*. Paris: Études augustiniennes.

Mandouze, André, and Anne-Marie La Bonnardière. 1982. *Prosopographie de l'Afrique chrétienne (303–533)*. Prosopographie Chrétienne du Bas-Empire 1. Paris: Éditions du Centre National de la Recherche Scientifique.

Markus, Robert A. 1970. *Saeculum: History and Society in the Theology of St. Augustine*. Cambridge: Cambridge University Press.

———. 1990. *The End of Ancient Christianity*. Cambridge: Cambridge University Press.

———. 2010. "The Secular in Late Antiquity." In *Les frontières du profane dans l'antiquité tardive*, edited by Éric Rebillard and Claire Sotinel, 353–361. Collection de l'École Française de Rome 428. Rome: École Française de Rome.

Marrou, Henri-Irénée. 1977. "Problèmes généraux de l'onomastique chrétienne." In *L'onomastique latine: Actes du Colloque international sur l'onomastique latine, Paris, 13–15 octobre*, edited by Noël Duval, 431–435. Paris: Centre National de la Recherche Scientifique.

Martin, Dale B., and Patricia Cox Miller, eds. 2005. *The Cultural Turn in Late Ancient Studies: Gender, Asceticism, and Historiography*. Durham, NC: Duke University Press.

Mason, Steve. 2007. "Jews, Judaeans, Judaizing, Judaism: Problems of Categorization in Ancient History." *Journal for the Study of Judaism (in the Persian, Hellenistic, and Roman Period)* 38 (4–5): 457–512.

Mastandrea, Paolo, ed., trans., and annot. 1985. *Massimo di Madauros, Agostino, Epistulae 16 e 17*. Saggi e Materiali Universitari. Serie Di Antichità e Tradizione Classica. Padua: Editoriale Programma.

Mattei, Paul. 1990. "Le schisme de Tertullien: Essai de mise au point biographique et ecclésiologique." In *Hommage à René Braun*, vol. 2, *Autour de Tertullien*, edited by Jean Granarolo and Michèle Biraud, 129–149. Paris: Les Belles Lettres.

———. 2000. "L'ecclésiologie de Tertullien: Bilan provisoire." In *Anthropos Laïkos: Mélanges Alexandre Faivre à l'occasion de ses 30 ans d'enseignement*, edited by Marie-Anne Vannier, Otto Wermelinger, and Gregor Wurst, 162–178. Fribourg: Editions Universitaires.

———. 2007. "Les frontières de l'Église selon la première tradition africaine (Tertullien, Cyprien, Anonyme du *De Rebaptismate*)." *Revue des sciences religieuses* 81 (1): 27–47.

Matthews, John F. 1974. "The Letters of Symmachus." In *Latin Literature of the Fourth Century*, edited by James W. Binns, 58–99. London: Routledge and Kegan Paul.

Maxwell, Jaclyn L. 2006. *Christianization and Communication in Late Antiquity: John Chrysostom and His Congregation in Antioch*. Cambridge: Cambridge University Press.

McCall, George J., and Jerry L. Simmons. 1966. *Identities and Interactions*. New York: Free Press.

———. 1978. *Identities and Interactions: An Examination of Human Associations in Everyday Life*. Rev ed. New York: Free Press.

McGowan, Andrew. 2003. "Discipline and Diet: Feeding the Martyrs in Roman Carthage." *Harvard Theological Review* 96 (4): 455–476.

———. 2004. "Rethinking Agape and Eucharist in Early North African Christianity." *Studia liturgica* 34: 165–176.

McLynn, Neil B. 1999. "Augustine's Roman Empire." *Augustinian Studies* 30 (2): 29–44.

———. 2009. "Pagans in a Christian Empire." In *A Companion to Late Antiquity*, edited by Philip Rousseau and Jutta Raithel, 572–587. Chichester, UK: Wiley-Blackwell.

Meckler, Michael Louis. 1994. "Caracalla and His Late-Antique Biographer: A Historical Commentary on the Vita Caracalli in the Historia Augusta." PhD diss., University of Michigan.

Meslin, Michel. 1970. *La fête des kalendes de janvier dans l'Empire romain: Étude d'un rituel de nouvel an*. Collection Latomus 115. Brussels: Editions Latomus.

Micaelli, Claudio, and Charles Munier, ed., trans., and annot. 1993. *Tertullien, La pudicité*. Sources Chrétiennes 394–395. Paris: Éditions du Cerf.

Mitchell, Margaret Mary, Frances M. Young, and K. Scott Bowie, eds. 2006. *The Cambridge History of Christianity*. Vol. 1, *Origins to Constantine*. Cambridge: Cambridge University Press.

Mitchell, Stephen. 1988. "Maximinus and the Christians in A.D. 312: A New Latin Inscription." *Journal of Roman Studies* 78: 105–124.

Monceaux, Paul. 1901–23. *Histoire littéraire de l'Afrique chrétienne depuis les origines jusqu'à l'invasion arabe*. 6 vols. Paris: E. Leroux.

Moreau, Madeleine. 1973. *Le dossier Marcellinus dans la correspondance de saint Augustin*. Paris: Études Augustiniennes.

———. 1998. "Le magistrat et l'évêque: Pour une lecture de la correspondance Macedonius-Augustin." In *Curiosité historique et intérets philologiques: Hommage à Serge Lancel*, edited by Bernard Colombat and Paul Mattei, 105–117. Grenoble: Université Stendhal-Grenoble.

Morgenstern, Frank. 1993. *Die Briefpartner des Augustinus von Hippo: Prosopographische, sozial- und ideologiegeschichtliche Untersuchungen*. Bochumer Historische Studien. Alte Geschichte 11. Bochum: Universitätsverlag Dr. N. Brockmeyer.

Musurillo, Herbert, trans. 1972. *The Acts of the Christian Martyrs*. Oxford Early Christian Texts. Oxford: Clarendon Press.
Nicholson, Oliver. 1989. "Flight from Persecution as Imitation of Christ: Lactantius' Divine Institutes IV. 18. 1–2." *Journal of Theological Studies* 40 (1): 48–65.
———. 2009. "Preparation for Martyrdom in the Early Church." In *The Great Persecution: The Proceedings of the Fifth Patristic Conference, Maynooth, 2003*, edited by Vincent D. Twomey and Mark Humphries, 61–90. Dublin: Four Courts Press.
Nock, Arthur Darby. 1933. *Conversion, the Old and the New in Religion from Alexander the Great to Augustine of Hippo*. Donnellan Lectures, 1931; Lowell Institute Lectures, 1933. London: Oxford University Press.
North, John A. 1992. "The Development of Religious Pluralism." In *The Jews among Pagans and Christians: In the Roman Empire*, edited by Judith Lieu, John North, and Tessa Rajak, 174–193. London: Routledge.
———. 2000. *Roman Religion*. Greece & Rome 30. Oxford: Oxford University Press.
O'Donnell, James J. 2005. *Augustine: A New Biography*. New York: Ecco.
Olivar, Alexandre. 1991. *La predicación cristiana antigua*. Biblioteca Herder. Sección de Teología y Filosofía 189. Barcelona: Herder.
Oliveira, Júlio César Magalhães de. 2004. "Le pouvoir du peuple: Une émeute à Hippone au début du Ve siècle connue par le sermon 302 de saint Augustin pour la fête de saint Laurent." *Antiquité tardive* 12: 309–324.
———. 2006. "*Vt Maiores Pagani Non Sint!* Pouvoir, iconoclasme et action populaire à Carthage au début du Ve siècle (saint Augustin, Sermons 24, 279 et Morin 1)." *Antiquité tardive* 14: 245–262.
O'Malley, Thomas P. 1967. *Tertullian and the Bible: Language, Imagery, Exegesis*. Latinitas Christianorum Primaeva 21. Nijmegen: Dekker & Van de Vegt.
Pagels, Elaine H. 1980. "Gnostic and Orthodox Views of Christ's Passion: Paradigms for the Christian's Response to Persecution?" In *The Rediscovery of Gnosticism: Proceedings of the International Conference on Gnosticism at Yale, New Haven, Connecticut, March 28–31, 1978*, edited by Bentley Layton, 262–283. Leiden: Brill.
Pavón, Pilar. 1999. "Régimen de vida y tratamiento del preso durante los tres primeros siglos del imperio." In *Carcer: Prison et privation de liberté dans l'antiquité classique; Actes du Colloque de Strasbourg, 5 et 6 décembre 1997*, edited by Cécile Bertrand-Dagenbach, 105–113. Paris: De Boccard.
Penn, Michael Philip. 2005. *Kissing Christians: Ritual and Community in the Late Ancient Church*. Divinations: Rereading Ancient Religion. Philadelphia: University of Pennsylvania Press.
Perkins, Judith. 2009. *Roman Imperial Identities in the Early Christian Era*. Routledge Monographs in Classical Studies. London: Routledge.
Perler, Othmar. 1969. *Les voyages de saint Augustin*. Collection des Études Augustiniennes. Série Antiquité 36. Paris: Études Augustiniennes.
Perrin, Michel-Yves. 2010. "*Crevit hypocrisis*: Limites d'adhésion au christianisme dans l'antiquité tardive, entre histoire et historiographie." In *Le problème de la christianisation du monde antique*, edited by Hervé Inglebert, Sylvain Destephen, and Bruno Dumézil, 47–62. Paris: Picard.
Pétré, Hélène. 1948. *Caritas: Étude sur le vocabulaire latin de la charité chrétienne*. Études et Documents 22. Louvain: Spicilegium Sacrum Lovaniense.

Petropoulou, Maria-Zoe. 2008. *Animal Sacrifice in Ancient Greek Religion, Judaism, and Christianity, 100 BC–AD 200.* Oxford: Oxford University Press.

Picard, Gilbert-Charles. 1990. *La civilisation de l'Afrique romaine.* Paris: Études Augustiniennes.

Pietri, Charles. 1977. "Remarques sur l'onomastique chrétienne de Rome." In *L'onomastique latine: Actes du colloque international sur l'onomastique latine, Paris, 13–15 octobre 1975,* edited by Noël Duval, 437–445. Paris: Centre National de la Recherche Scientifique.

———. 1997. *Christiana Respublica: Éléments d'une enquête sur le christianisme antique.* 3 vols. Collection de l'École Française de Rome 234. Rome: École Française de Rome.

Poque, Suzanne. 1987. "Un souci pastoral d'Augustin: La persévérance des chrétiens baptisés dans leur enfance." *Bulletin de littérature ecclésiastique* 88: 273–286.

Poschmann, Bernhard. 1964. *Penance and the anointing of the sick.* Translated by Francis Courtney. London: Burns & Oates.

Quasten, Johannes. 1940. "*Vetus superstitio et nova religio*: The Problem of Refrigerium in the Ancient Church of North Africa." *Harvard Theological Review* 33: 253–266.

Quentin, Henri. 1908. *Les martyrologes historiques du Moyen Age: Étude sur la formation du Martyrologe romain.* Études d'Histoire des Dogmes et d'Ancienne Littérature Ecclésiastique. Paris: Lecoffre.

Rajak, Tessa. 2009. *Translation and Survival: The Greek Bible of the Ancient Jewish Diaspora.* Oxford: Oxford University Press.

Rankin, David. 1995. *Tertullian and the Church.* Cambridge: Cambridge University Press.

Rebillard, Éric. 1994. *In hora mortis: Évolution de la pastorale chrétienne de la mort aux IVe et Ve siècles dans l'Occident latin.* Bibliothèque des Écoles Françaises d'Athènes et de Rome 283. Rome: École Française de Rome.

———. 1996. "Les areae carthaginoises (Tertullien, *Ad Scapulam* 3, 1): Cimetières communautaires ou enclos funéraires de chrétiens?" *Mélanges de l'École française de Rome, Antiquité* 108 (1): 175–189.

———. 1997. "Interaction between the Preacher and His Audience: The Case-Study of Augustine's Preaching on Death." In *Studia Patristica,* vol. 31, *Papers Presented at the Twelfth International Conference on Patristic Studies Held in Oxford, 1995,* edited by Elizabeth A. Livingstone, 86–96. Leuven: Peeters.

———. 1998. "La figure du catéchumène et le problème du délai du baptême dans la pastorale d'Augustin." In *Augustin prédicateur (395–411): Actes du Colloque international de Chantilly (5–7 septembre 1996),* edited by Goulven Madec, 285–292. Collection des Études Augustiniennes. Série Antiquité 159. Paris: Institut d'Études Augustiniennes, 1998.

———. 2005. "*Nec deserere memorias suorum:* Augustine and the Family-Based Commemoration of the Dead." *Augustinian Studies* 36 (1): 99–111.

———. 2009a. "Augustin et le culte des statues." In *Ministerium Sermonis: Philological, Historical, and Theological Studies on Augustine's Sermones ad Populum,* edited by Gert Partoens, Anthony Dupont, and Mathijs Lamberigts, 299–325. Turnhout: Brepols.

———. 2009b. *The Care of the Dead in Late Antiquity*. Translated by Elizabeth Trapnell Rawlings and Jeanine Routier-Pucci. Cornell Studies in Classical Philology 59. Ithaca, NY: Cornell University Press.

———. 2010. "Vivre avec les païens, mais non mourir avec eux: Le problème de la commensalité des chrétiens et des non-chrétiens (Ier-Ve siècles)." In *Les frontières du profane dans l'antiquité tardive*, edited by Éric Rebillard and Claire Sotinel, 151–176. Collection de l'École Française de Rome 428. Rome: École Française de Rome.

———. Forthcoming. "Peuple chrétien et destruction des statues pai ennes: le dossier africain à la lumière des textes d'Augustin." In *Faire parler et faire taire les statues*, edited by Yann Rivière. Rome: École Française de Rome.

Rebillard, Éric, and Claire Sotinel, eds. 2010. *Les frontières du profane dans l'antiquité tardive*. Collection de l'École Française de Rome 428. Rome: École Française de Rome.

Rives, James B. 1995. *Religion and Authority in Roman Carthage from Augustus to Constantine*. Oxford: Clarendon Press.

———. 1996. "The Piety of a Persecutor." *Journal of Early Christian Studies* 4 (1): 1–25.

———. 1999. "The Decree of Decius and the Religion of Empire." *Journal of Roman Studies* 89: 135–154.

Rivière, Yann. 2002. *Les délateurs sous l'Empire romain*. Bibliothèque des Écoles Françaises d'Athènes et de Rome 311. Rome: École Française de Rome.

Rousseau, Philip. 1998. "The Preacher's Audience: A More Optimistic View." In *Ancient History in a Modern University*, vol. 2, *Early Christianity, Late Antiquity and Beyond*, edited by T. W. Hillard, R. A. Kearsley, C. E. V. Nixon, and A. M. Nobbs, 391–400. Grand Rapids, MI: Eerdmans.

Rousset, Jean. 1962. *Forme et signification: Essais sur les structures littéraires de Corneille à Claudel*. Paris: Corti.

Ruggiero, Fabio. 1988. "Il problema del numero dei martiri Scilitani." *Cristianesimo nella storia* 9: 135–152.

———. ed., trans., and annot. 1991. *Atti dei martiri Scilitani*. Memorie 1/2. Rome: Accademia Nazionale dei Lincei.

Rüpke, Jörg. 2009. "Early Christianity out of, and in, Context." *Journal of Roman Studies* 99: 182–193.

———. 2010. "Religious Pluralism." In *Oxford Handbook of Roman Studies*, edited by Alessandro Barchiesi and Walter Scheidel, 748–766. Oxford: Oxford University Press.

Sage, Michael M. 1975. *Cyprian*. Patristic Monograph Series 1. Cambridge, MA: Philadelphia Patristic Foundation.

Salzman, Michele Rene. 2006. "Rethinking Pagan-Christian Violence." In *Violence in Late Antiquity: Perceptions and Practices*, edited by Harold A. Drake, 265–285. Aldershot, UK: Ashgate.

Sandwell, Isabella. 2007. *Religious Identity in Late Antiquity: Greeks, Jews, and Christians in Antioch*. Greek Culture in the Roman World. Cambridge: Cambridge University Press.

Saumagne, Charles. 1975. *Saint Cyprien, évêque de Carthage, "Pape" d'Afrique, 248–258: Contribution à l'étude des "persécutions" de Dèce et de Valérien*. Études d'Antiquités Africaines. Paris: Éditions du Centre National de la Recherche Scientifique.

Saxer, Victor. 1988. *Les rites de l'initiation chrétienne du IIe au VIe siècle.* Centro Italiano di Studi sull'Alto Medioevo 7. Spoleto: Centro Italiano di Studi sull'Alto Medioevo.
Scheid, John. 1998. "Les réjouissances des calendes de janvier d'après le sermon Dolbeau 26: Nouvelles lumières sur une fête mal connue." In *Augustin prédicateur (395–411): Actes du Colloque international de Chantilly (5–7 septembre 1996),* edited by Goulven Madec, 353–365. Paris: Institut d'Études Augustiniennes.
Schindler, Alfred. 2003. "Du nouveau sur les donatistes au temps de Saint Augustin?" In *Augustinus Afer: Saint Augustin, africanité et universalité,* edited by Pierre-Yves Fux, Jean-Michel Roessli, and Otto Wermelinger, 1: 149–152. Fribourg: Editions Universitaires.
Schöllgen, Georg. 1982. "Die Teilnahme der Christen am städtischen Leben in vorkonstantinischer Zeit: Tertullians Zeugnis für Karthago." *Römische Quartalschrift* 77 (1–2): 1–29.
———. 1985. *Ecclesia Sordida? Zur Frage der sozialen Schichtung frühchristlicher Gemeinden am Beispiel Karthagos zur Zeit Tertullians.* Jahrbuch für Antike und Christentum. Ergänzungsband 12. Münster: Aschendorff.
Schwarte, Karl-Heinz. 1994. "Diokletians Christengesetz." In *E fontibus haurire: Beiträge zur römischen Geschichte und zu ihren Hilfswissenschaften,* edited by Heinrich Chantraine, Rosmarie Günther, and Stefan Rebenich, 203–240. Paderborn: Schöningh.
Schwartz, Seth. 2001. *Imperialism and Jewish Society, 200 B.C.E. to 640 C.E.* Jews, Christians, and Muslims from the Ancient to the Modern World. Princeton, NJ: Princeton University Press.
Scott, Joan Wallach. 2007. *The Politics of the Veil.* The Public Square Book Series. Princeton, NJ: Princeton University Press.
Selinger, Reinhard. 2002. *The Mid-Third-Century Persecutions of Decius and Valerian.* Frankfurt am Main: Lang.
Sen, Amartya. 2006. *Identity and Violence: The Illusion of Destiny.* Issues of Our Time. New York: Norton & Co.
Sewell, William Hamilton. 2005. *Logics of History: Social Theory and Social Transformation.* Chicago Studies in Practices of Meaning. Chicago: University of Chicago Press.
Shaw, Brent D. 2011. *Sacred Violence: African Christians and Sectarian Hatred in the Age of Augustine.* Cambridge: Cambridge University Press.
Simmons, Michael Bland. 1995. *Arnobius of Sicca: Religious Conflict and Competition in the Age of Diocletian.* Oxford: Clarendon Press.
Sizgorich, Thomas. 2009. *Violence and Belief in Late Antiquity: Militant Devotion in Christianity and Islam.* Divinations: Rereading Ancient Religion. Philadelphia: University of Pennsylvania Press.
Smith, Wilfred Cantwell. 1963. *The Meaning and End of Religion: A New Approach to the Religious Traditions of Mankind.* New York: Macmillan.
Soler, Emmanuel. 2010a. "Les 'demi-chrétiens' d'Antioche: La pédagogie de l'exclusivisme chrétien et ses ressorts dans la prédication chrysostomienne." In *Le problème de la christianisation du monde antique,* edited by Hervé Inglebert, Sylvain Destephen, and Bruno Dumézil, 281–291. Paris: Picard.

———. 2010b. "Sacralité et partage du temps et de l'espace festifs à Antioche au IVe siècle." In *Les frontières du profane dans l'antiquité tardive*, edited by Éric Rebillard and Claire Sotinel, 273–286. Collection de l'École Française de Rome 428. Rome: École Française de Rome.
Spiegel, Gabrielle M. 1990. "History, Historicism, and the Social Logic of the Text in the Middle Ages." *Speculum* 65 (1): 59–86.
———. 2005. *Practicing History: New Directions in Historical Writing after the Linguistic Turn*. Rewriting Histories. New York: Routledge.
Spiro, Melford E. 1993. "Is the Western Conception of the Self 'Peculiar' within the Context of World Cultures?" *Ethos* 21 (2): 107–153.
Stowers, Stanley. 2011. "The Concept of 'Community' and the History of Early Christianity." *Method and Theory in the Study of Religion* 23: 238–256.
Stroumsa, Guy G. 1998. "Tertullian on idolatry and the limits of tolerance." In *Tolerance and Intolerance in Early Judaism and Christianity*, edited by Graham N. Stanton and Guy G. Stroumsa, 173–184. Cambridge: Cambridge University Press.
Tabbernee, William. 2001. "To Pardon or Not to Pardon? North African Montanism and the Forgiveness of Sins." *Studia Patristica,* vol. 36, *Papers presented at the Thirteenth International Conference on Patristic Studies held in Oxford 1999,* edited by Maurice F. Wiles and E. J. Yarnold, 375–386. Leuven: Peeters.
———. 2007. *Fake Prophecy and Polluted Sacraments: Ecclesiastical and Imperial Reactions to Montanism*. Supplements to Vigiliae Christianae 84. Leiden: Brill.
Tels-de Jong, Leontine Louise. 1959. *Sur quelques divinités romaines de la naissance et de la prophétie*. Delft: Grafisch Bedrijf Avanti.
Thomassen, Einar. 2006. *The Spiritual Seed: The Church of the "Valentinians."* Nag Hammadi and Manichaean Studies 60. Leiden: Brill.
Tilley, Maureen A. 1997. *The Bible in Christian North Africa: The Donatist World*. Minneapolis: Fortress Press.
Trevett, Christine. 1996. *Montanism: Gender, Authority, and the New Prophecy*. Cambridge: Cambridge University Press.
Trout, Dennis E. 1999. *Paulinus of Nola: Life, Letters, and Poems*. The Transformation of the Classical Heritage 27. Berkeley: University of California Press.
Turcan, Marie, ed., trans., and annot. 1986. *Tertullien, Les spectacles*. Sources Chrétiennes 332. Paris: Éditions du Cerf.
Uhalde, Kevin. 2007. *Expectations of Justice in the Age of Augustine*. Philadelphia: University of Pennsylvania Press.
Urbach, Ephraim E. 1959. "The Rabbinical Laws of Idolatry in the Second and Third Centuries in the Light of Archaeological and Historical Facts." *Israel Exploration Journal* 9 (3): 149–165 and (4): 229–245.
Van der Lof, Johan L. 1981. "The Threefold Meaning of *Servi Dei* in the Writings of Saint Augustine." *Augustinian Studies* 12: 43–59.
———. 1991. "The Plebs of the Psychici: Are the Psychici of *De Monogamia* Fellow-Catholics of Tertullian?" In *Eulogia: Mélanges offerts à Antoon A. R. Bastiaensen à l'occasion de son soixante-cinquième anniversaire,* edited by Gerardus J. M. Bartelink, Antonius Hilhorst, and C. H. Kneepkens, 353–363. The Hague: Nijhoff.

Van der Meer, Frederik. 1961. *Augustine the Bishop: Religion and Society at the Dawn of the Middle Ages*. Translated by Brian Battershaw and G. R. Lamb. New York: Harper & Row.

Van der Nat, Pieter G. 1964. "Tertullianea. II. The Structure of the *De spectaculis*" *Vigiliae Christianae* 18: 129–143.

Van Winden, J. C. M. 1982. "*Idolum* and *Idololatria* in Tertullian." *Vigiliae Christianae* 36: 108–114.

Waltzing, Jean-Pierre. 1912. "La thèse de J.-B. De Rossi sur les collèges funéraires chrétiens." *Bulletin de l'Académie royale de Belgique* 6: 387–401.

Wankenne, Ludovic-Jules. 1974. "À propos de Dioscorus, correspondant de saint Augustin (*Epist.* CXVII-CXVIII)." *Revue bénédictine* 84: 167–176.

Waszink Jan H., and Jacobus C. M. Van Winden, ed., trans., and annot. 1987. *Tertullian, De Idololatria*. Supplements to Vigiliae Christianae 1. Leiden: Brill.

Watzlawick, Paul, Janet Helmick Beavin, and Don D. Jackson. 1967. *Pragmatics of Human Communication: A Study of Interactional Patterns, Pathologies, and Paradoxes*. 1st ed. New York: Norton.

White, Lloyd Michael. 1996. *The Social Origins of Christian Architecture*. 2 vols. Harvard Theological Studies 42–43. Valley Forge, PA: Trinity Press International.

Wilmart, André. 1931. "Operum S. Augustini elenchus a Possidio eiusdem discipulo Calamensi episcopo digestus." In *Miscellanea Agostiniana: Testi e studi pubblicati a cura dell' Ordine eremitano di s. Agostino nel xv centenario dalla morte del santo dottore*, 2: 149–233. Rome: Tipografica Poliglotta Vaticana.

Yasin, Ann Marie. 2009. *Saints and Church Spaces in the Late Antique Mediterranean: Architecture, Cult, and Community*. Greek Culture in the Roman World. Cambridge: Cambridge University Press.

Zumkeller, Adolar. 1991. "Der Gebrauch der Termini *famulus Dei, servus Dei, serva Dei* und *ancilla Dei* bei Augustinus." In *Eulogia: Mélanges offerts à Antoon A. R. Bastiaensen à l'occasion de son soixante-cinquième anniversaire*, edited by Gerardus J. M. Bartelink, Antonius Hilhorst, and C. H. Kneepkens, 437–445. The Hague: Nijhoff.

Index

abstention, Christians recognized by, 18–20
Acts of Cyprian, 57
Acts of Felix of Thibiuca, 59
Acts of Gallonius, 59
Acts of Martyrs, 42, 43
Acts of the Martyrs of Abithina, 59
Acts of the Scillitan Martyrs, 35–36
Aemilius, martyrdom of, 101n14
agape (weekly evening gathering), 15
Agrippinus (bishop of Carthage), 10
Albina (mother of Melania the Younger), 81, 105n18
Alfius Caecilianus, 59
apostasy
 Edict of Decius, Christians compliant with, 50–51, 54
 Tertullian's condemnation of flight and bribery as forms of, 46
Arnobius, 6, 60, 69
Arrius Antoninus (proconsul of Asia), 41
Aspasius Paternus (proconsul of Africa), 55
Asper (C. Julius Asper, proconsul of Africa), 40
ass's head, Christian God portrayed with, 37
astrology, 26, 66, 67, 73, 75, 104n7
Augustine
 and Christian identity, 8, 61–91
 category membership sets, arrangement of, 78–79, 84, 105n25
 churchgoing/Mass attendance, 66, 67–68
 City of God, 84
 civic identity, 77–78, 83–84
 client-patron relationships, 76–77, 78
 collective Christian action. *See under* collective Christian action
 Commentary on Galatians, 66
 Confessions, 64, 70
 criminals, episcopal intercession on behalf of, 84–85
 De catechizandis rudibus, 64, 65, 67
 definition of Christian membership, 64–67
 dualism of temporal and eternal life, 71–73

education, early career, and social status of Augustine, letters referencing, 79–82, 84, 85
evidence regarding, 5, 7, 62–64
external markers of Christianness, lack of, 67
gift-giving at traditional celebrations, 78
laypeople and clergy, different behavioral standards for, 73
in letter exchanges, 62–63, 79–85
 with Dioscorus, 79–81
 with Macedonius, 84–85
 with Nectarius, 82–84
 with Volusianus, 81–82
life-cycle rituals, Christian ceremonies marking, 68–70
magical practices, Christian engagement in, 72–73, 74–75
multiple identities of individuals, 3–5, 74, 85, 91
pagan and Christian in society, changed balance of, 61–62
priority/singularity of Christian identity, Augustine's promotion of, 74, 75, 77, 79, 80, 82, 85, 91, 92
scriptural legalism, 70–71
"secular" and "religious," dichotomous concepts of, 62, 91
sermons of Augustine, 63
sickbeds, ritual practices at, 74–75
Sufes riot, 86–87
temples, Christian attendance at, 76–77
theatergoing, 66, 77–78
Aurelius (bishop of Carthage), 70, 89
Ausonius, 69
Avodah Zarah, 94
avoidance of persecution. *See* evasion of persecution
Aziza, Claude, 37

baptism, 11, 12, 64, 65, 67, 75, 81, 83
Barnes, Timothy, 9, 11, 35, 44, 47, 56–57, 57–58, 60, 103n36

INDEX

The Beginnings of Jewishness (Cohen, 1999), 13
Birley, Anthony, 35, 38, 41
bishops and clergy
   Calama riots, clergy involvement in, 87–88, 106n28
   criminals, intercession on behalf of, 84–85
   in Diocletian's persecution, 58, 59
   laypeople's social and civic obligations versus, 73
   at marriage and burial ceremonies, 69
   as public figures, 49
   in Tertullian's Carthage, 10
   in Valerian's persecution, 55–56
Bonifatius (bishop), 84
Bonner, Gerald, 95
Boyarin, Daniel, 93–94
Braun, René, 43
Brent, Allen, 50–51
Breuiarium Hipponense, 73
bribery to avoid persecution, 46, 51
Brown, Peter, 61, 73, 96
Brubaker, Rogers, 3–4, 106n1
Brumae, festival of, 28
Bulla Reggia, 61, 73, 77–78
burials and burial sites
   attacks on Christian burial sites, 16–17, 37
   Christian gatherings at, 16–17
   Christian practices regarding, 69, 70
   funerary associations, 32–33
   meals at, 70–71
   parentalia, 71
   prohibition on Christian assembly during Valerian persecution, 55
Burke, Peter, 4

Caecilianus (bishop of Carthage), 59
Calama riots, 84–85, 87–88, 106n28
Calends of January, 28, 78
Calends of June, 87
Cameron, Alan, 81, 95
Candidus (Vespronius Candidus, legate of the III Augusta), 36, 101n6
Cantwell, Wilfred, 94
Caracalla (Roman emperor), 9, 48
Carthage
   conversion of Faustinus at, 89–90
   Council of Carthage (397), 73
   genius of, 77
   persecution of Christians in. *See* persecution and Christian identity
   "shaving of Hercules" at, 88–89
   in Tertullian's time, 7, 9–33
Castus, martyrdom of, 101n14
catechumens, 11, 12, 64–66, 69, 81, 83

category membership sets, arrangement of, 4–5, 78–79, 84, 105n25
celebrations. *See* festivities, Christian engagement in
Celerina, martyrdom of, 47
Celerinus, 47
cemeteries. *See* burials and burial sites
center-pagans and center-Christians, as categories, 95
charitable activities of Christians
   martyrs in prison, support of, 16, 33, 39–40, 43, 52–53
   mutual social assistance between Christians, 32–33
   poor, help for, 16, 32–33, 78
Christian identity in late antique North Africa, 1–8, 92–97
   Augustine and, 8, 61–91. *See also* Augustine and Christian identity
   burials and cemeteries. *See* burials and burial sites
   category membership sets, arrangement of, 4–5, 78–79, 84, 105n25
   Constantinian revolution/Peace of the Church as major point in Christian history, 59–60, 95, 96–97
   discursive constructs of, 1, 5–6
   evidence regarding, 5–6
   "groupism," avoiding, 1–3
   groupness and collective Christian action. *See* collective Christian action
   individuals, multiple identities, and identity theory, 3–5, 74, 85, 91, 92–93, 95
   under persecution, 7–8, 34–60. *See also* persecution and Christian identity
   pre-Constantinian and Theodosian periods, need for comparison of, 60, 97
   problem, Christian life in pagan society viewed as, 9, 31
   religious pluralism and, 62, 93–94
   "secular" and "religious," dichotomous concepts of, 62, 91, 95–96
   "semi-Christians," concept of, 94–95, 107n4
   in Tertullian's Carthage, 7, 9–33. *See also* Tertullian
churchgoing/Mass attendance
   in Augustine's time, 66, 67–68
   Eucharist, 15, 68, 69, 71
   prohibitions on Christian assembly, 55, 58, 59
   Tertullian's Carthage, liturgical events in, 15–16, 100n4–5

INDEX

Cicero, 80
Cingius Severus (proconsul of Africa), 36
civic identity and Christian identity, 77–78, 83–84
Clarke, Graeme W., 49, 50
clergy. *See* bishops and clergy
client-patron relationships in late antique North Africa, 76–77, 78
Clodius Albinus, defeat of, 38
clothing, Tertullian's awareness of significance of, 13, 23–25
Cohen, Shaye, 13, 14
collective Christian action
   in Augustinian North Africa, 86–91
      Calama riots, 87–88
      Faustinus, reaction to conversion of, 89–90
      "shaving of Hercules" at Carthage, 88–89
      Sufes riot, 86–87
   groupness, Christianness as basis for, 86, 90–91, 93
   persecution, in response to
      Edict of Decius, Cyprian's efforts to avoid collective targeting of Christians under, 53–55, 60
      execution of Cyprian, crowd response to, 57
      in Tertullian's Carthage, 41–42, 43–47
      Valerian's persecution, possible Christian riot due to, 56–57
collective versus individualistic personality, 99n6
committed pagans and committed Christians, as categories, 95
confessions of faith in response to Edict of Decius, 52–53
Constantine I (Roman emperor), 58, 60
Constantinian revolution/Peace of the Church, 59–60, 95, 96–97
conversion
   Augustinian process not common to all Christians, 70
   of Faustinus, 89–90
   Tertullian on gossip about conversion of individual Christians, 17
Cornelius (bishop of Rome), 103n31
criminals, episcopal intercession on behalf of, 84–85
Cyprian (bishop of Carthage)
   bishops of Carthage prior to, 10
   death as martyr, 35, 55, 56–57
   Edict of Decius and
      different Christian responses to, 50–55
      efforts to avoid collective targeting of Christians, 53–55, 60
      in hiding in response to, 48–49, 52, 55
      evidence provided by, 6, 47
      liturgical events in Carthage of, 100n5
      on "long peace" before Edict of Decius, 47
      popular hostility against Christians related by, 48–50
   in Valerian's persecution, 55

Daguet-Gagey, Anne, 39, 101n10
De Rossi, Giovanni Battista, 32
de Ste. Croix, Geoffrey, 53, 58
Decius, Edict of (250). *See* Edict of Decius
delator, 34, 43
denunciations of Christians, 34, 42
Diocletian, Edict of (Great Persecution; 303), *See* Edict of Diocletian
Diogenes the Cynic, 22
Dionysius, bishop of Alexandria, 13
Dioscorus (correspondent of Augustine), 79–81
discursive constructs, 1, 5–6
"documentary model," 5–6
Dolbeau, François, 56, 63, 68
Donatists, 6–7, 58, 59, 60, 63, 101n8, 104n3
Dossey, Leslie, 64
dualism of temporal and eternal life, 71–73

Ebbeler, Jen, 62
Edict of Decius (250), 7, 47–55
   Christian responses to, 50–55
      collective targeting of Christians, efforts to avoid, 53–55, 60
      compliance by majority of Christians, 50–51, 54, 60
      confession, 52–53
      false certificates and bribes, 51–52
      flight, 52–53
      stantes (neither sacrificing nor confessing), 53
      turificati (offering only incense), 103n31
   Christians probably not intentional target of, 34, 47, 48, 55
   Cyprian and. *See under* Cyprian
   intent, form, and implementation, 47–48
   popular hostility against Christians and, 48–50, 54, 55
Edict of Diocletian (Great Persecution; 303), 6, 58–59
Edict of Gallienus (260), 57–58, 59
Edict of Milan (313), 58

education
    Augustine's education, early career, and social status, letters referencing, 79–82, 84, 85
    of Christians, 26, 31–32
    teaching, as Christian occupation, 26
Egnatius, martyrdom of, 47
The End of Ancient Christianity (Markus, 1990), 95–96
Eucharist, 15, 68, 69, 71
Eusebius of Caesarea, 13, 34, 58
evasion of persecution
    by Christians under Edict of Decius, 50–52, 54–55
    by Christians under Edict of Diocletian, 58, 59
    Tertullian's discouragement of, 44–45, 46
excommunicati, 67
external markers of Christianness, lack of, 13–14, 67

Fabius (in Tertullian's *De fuga*), 45
the faithful, versus catechumens, 65–66
Faustinus, conversion of, 89–90
Felicity and Perpetua, martyrdom of, 16, 17, 38–40
Felix, bishop of Abthugni, 59
festivities, Christian engagement in
    genius of Carthage, Augustine on celebration of, 77
    gift-giving at traditional celebrations, Augustine on, 78
    life-cycle rituals, Christian ceremonies marking, 68–70
    ludi, Christian participation in/abstention from, 14, 19, 20–23, 27–29, 73
    public and private non-Christian celebrations, Tertullian on, 27–29, 68–70
    "secular" and "religious," dichotomous concepts of, 96
    theatergoing, Augustine's condemnation of, 66, 77–78
flight from persecution, 46, 52
Flint, Valerie, 72–73
Franchi de' Cavalieri, Pio, 56
funerary associations in Roman empire, 32–33
funerary practices. *See* burials and burial sites

Galerius Maximus (proconsul of Africa), 56–57
Gallienus (Roman emperor), 55, 57–58, 59
Gallus (Roman emperor), 49

Gaudentius (imperial emissary in Carthage), 86
genius of Carthage, celebration of, 77
Geta (son of Septimius Severus), 38, 40, 41
gift-giving at traditional celebrations, Augustine on, 78
gladiatorial games, Christian participation in/abstention from, 14, 19, 20–23, 27–29, 73
Gnostics and Gnosticism, 44, 45, 46, 47, 102n23
Great Persecution (Edict of Diocletian, 303), 6, 58–59
Grig, Lucy, 60
Groh, Dennis E., 31
group formation, Christianness as basis for. *See* collective Christian action
"groupism," 1–3
Guden, martyrdom of, 40, 102n15
Guignebert, Charles, 94–95

"habitus," 99n4
"halben Christen," 95
Hercules, statues of
    Carthage, "shaving of Hercules" at, 88–89
    Sufes riot and, 86–87
Hilarianus (P. Aelius Hilarianus), governor of Carthage, 16, 38–40
Hippo, Council of (393), 69
Histoire littéraire de l'Afrique chrétienne (Monceaux, 1901-23), 5
Hobsbawm, Eric, 3
holidays. *See* festivities, Christian engagement in
Honorius (Roman emperor), 86
Hopkins, Keith, 10
Hunter, David, 33

identity, Christian. *See* Christian identity in late antique North Africa
idol making, as occupation, 25–26
idol-meat, 32, 76
idolatry
    Jewish concepts of, 94
    temples, Augustine on Christian attendance at, 76–77
    Tertullian on what constitutes, 23, 25–31. *See also* Tertullian's *De Idololatria*
imperial cult, Christian abstention from, 19–20, 28
incerti, 95
individualistic versus collective personality, 99n6

individuals, multiple identities of, 3–5, 74, 85, 91, 92–93, 95
infant baptism, 65, 69
infant catechumens, 69

James, William, 4
Jerome, *De viris illustribus* 9–10
The Jews among Pagans and Christians: In the Roman Empire (Lieu, North, and Rajak, 1992), 3
John Chrysostom, 67, 105n25
Jovius (imperial emissary in Carthage), 86
Judaism, as religion, 94
Judaizing Christians, known as "semi-Christians," 107n4

Kahlos, Maijastina, 95
kiss as greeting amongst Christians, 17

LaCapra, Dominick, 5
Lactantius, 60
Lahire, Bernard, 3–4
Laurentinus, martyrdom of, 47
laypeople and clergy, different behavioral standards for, 73
Lepelley, Claude, 59, 62
libelli (false certificates of sacrifice), 51–52
Lieu, Judith, 2–3
Life of Melania the Younger, 81
liturgical events. *See* churchgoing/Mass attendance
"long peace" between end of reign of Septimius Severus and Edict of Decius, 47
ludi, Christian participation in/abstention from, 14, 19, 20–23, 27–29, 73

Macedonius (correspondent of Augustine), 84–85
MacMullen, Ramsay, 64, 70
Macrobius, 69
Madauros, martyrs of, 101n8
magical practices, Christian engagement in, 72–73, 74–75
Manichaeans, 63–64
Marcellinus (friend of Augustine), 80, 81
Marius the Epicurian (Pater, 1885), 103n43
Marius Victorinus, 64
Markus, Robert, 62, 95–96
marriage
  betrothals and weddings, non-Christian, Christian attendance at, 28–29
  Christian rituals of, 69
  between Christians and non-Christians, 11–12, 16, 18, 32
Martialis (Spanish bishop), 95
martyrs and martyrdom
  Augustine's promotion of adherence to Christian identity as, 74, 77
  persecutions. *See* persecution and Christian identity
Mass attendance. *See* churchgoing/Mass attendance
mass Christianization, phenomenon of, 95, 96
Matronalia, 28
Mavilus of Hadrumetum, martyrdom of, 42, 101n7, 102n16
Maxentius (Roman emperor), 58
McLynn, Neil, 83
Melania the Younger, 81, 105n19
Milan, Edict of (313), 58
military service, Christian involvement in, 29, 43–44, 58
Minor Peace of the Church (260-303), 57–58, 59
Minucius Felix, *Octavius* 18
Minucius Opimianus, 38, 102n15
Montanism (New Prophecy), 10, 44, 45
multiple identities of individuals, 3–5, 74, 85, 91, 92–93, 95

name-giving ceremonies, 68–69
names and naming conventions, Christian, 13, 67
Nectarius (correspondent of Augustine), 82–84, 87–88
New Prophecy (Montanism), 10, 44, 45
Nicholson, Oliver, 41
North, John A., 2–3, 93
Numidius, martyrdom of, 49–50
nuncupatio votorum, 48

oaths and swearing, 29–30
occupations of Christians, 13, 25–27, 32, 67
O'Donnell, Jim, 83
Optatus, bishop of Carthage, 10

pagan and Christian in society, change in balance of, 61–62
pagan celebrations. *See* festivities, Christian engagement in
pagan society, "problem" of Christian life in, 9, 31
pagan temples, Christian attendance at, 76–77

parentalia, 71
Passion of Perpetua and Felicitas, 16, 17, 38–40, 55, 57, 101n11
Passion of Lucius and Montanus, 55–57
Passion of Marian and James, 55–57
Pater, Walter, 103n43
patronage relationships in late antique North Africa, 76–77, 78
Peace of the Church, Constantinian, 59–60, 95, 96–97
penance and penitents, 12, 54, 67
Penn, Philip Michael, 17
Perpetua and Felicitas, martyrdom of, 16, 17, 38–40
Perrin, Michel-Yves, 97
persecution and Christian identity, 7–8, 34–60
 collective action due to. *See under* collective Christian action
 under Edict of Decius (250). *See* Edict of Decius
 evasion of persecution. *See* evasion of persecution
 Great Persecution (Edict of Diocletian, 303), 6, 58–59
 local governors, treatment of Christians mostly in hands of, 34
 "long peace" between end of reign of Septimius Severus and Edict of Decius, 47
 popular hatred of Christians. *See* popular hatred of Christians, claims of
 in Tertullian's Carthage, 35–47
  between 180 and 197, 35–36
  in 197-198, 36–38
  202-203, under Hilarianus, 38–40
  209-212, trials of Christians in, 40–41
  212-213, executions of, 40–42
  assemblies, harassment during, 14–15, 36, 46
  cemeteries of Christians, attacks on, 16–17
  charitable visits to imprisoned martyrs, 16, 33, 39–40
  collective Christian action in response to persecution, 41–42, 43–47
  denunciations, role of, 34, 42
  evasion of persecution, Tertullian's discouragement of, 44–45, 46
  flight and bribery condemned as forms of apostasy, 46
  popular hatred of Christians, claims of, 37–38, 39, 42–43
  potential impact on Carthaginian society, 11, 41–42
  stigmatization of Christians as a group, 37, 39
 Valerian's persecution (257-260), 55–57
Philip (Roman emperor), 47
philosophy and rhetoric, Augustine on, 79–82
plagues, 37, 49, 54
pollution, Christian beliefs about, 22–23
Pomponius (deacon), 39
Pontius, *Life of Cyprian*, 56, 57
poor
 Christian funeral banquets, invited to, 70
 Christian support for, 16, 32–33, 78
popular hatred of Christians, claims of
 Calama riots, 84–85, 87–88
 as Christian construct, 60
 Edict of Decius (250) and, 48–50, 54, 55
 Sufes riot, 86–87
 in Tertullian's works, 37–38, 39, 42–43
Poque, Suzanne, 65
Possidius, 67, 79, 84, 87, 88
proxy sacrificers, Christian use of, 51–52
psychici, 10
public games and festivals. *See* festivities, Christian involvement in
public worship of the gods, Christian abstention from, 18–20
Pudens (C. Valerius Pudens, governor), 40–41

Rajak, Tessa, 3
"religious" and "secular," dichotomous concepts of, 62, 91, 95–96
religious pluralism in late antique North Africa, 62, 93–94
Revocatus, martyrdom of, 39
rhetoric and philosophy, Augustine on, 79–82
Rives, James B., 19, 38, 39, 40, 48
Rufinus (Apuleius Rufinus, proconsul), 101–2n15
Rüpke, Jörg, 93

sacrifice on behalf of empire
 Decius's order requiring. *See* Edict of Decius
 Diocletian's order requiring, 58–59
Sage, Michael, 50
Sandwell, Isabella, 105n25
Saturnalia, 28
Saturus and Saturninus, martyrdom of, 39

Scapula (C. Julius [Scapula] Lepidus Tertullus; proconsul of Africa), 10–11, 41–42
schools and schooling. *See* education
Schwartz, Seth, 94
Scillitan martyrs, 35–36, 42
scriptures
  Christian use of, 22, 23–24, 70–71
  Diocletian's order requiring burning of, 58, 59
"secular" and "religious," dichotomous concepts of, 62, 91, 95–96
self-reflexivity, 99n4
"semi-Christians," concept of, 94–95, 107n4
Sen, Amartya, 107n6
Septimius Severus (Roman emperor), 9, 38–39, 40, 47
Shapur (Persian ruler), 57
Shaw, Brent, 106n37
sickbeds, ritual practices at, 74–75
sign of the cross *(signatio)*, 18, 64
Simittu, 78, 104n14
Simplicianus (presbyter of Milan), 64
Soler, Emmanuel, 107n4
spectacles, Christian participation in/abstention from, 14, 19, 20–23, 27–29, 73
speech, idolatry in, 29–30
Speratus (Scillitan martyr), 35–36
Spiegel, Gabrielle, 5
stantes, 53
Sufes, destruction of statue of Hercules at, 86–87
Sulpicius Severus, 47
supplicatio, 48
swearing and oaths, 29–30

tabulae matrimoniales, 69
teachers and teaching. *See* education
temples, Christian attendance at, 76–77
Tertius (deacon), 39
Tertullian
  abstentions, Christians recognized by, 18–20
  Ad martyras, 36, 43
  Ad nationes, 37
  Ad Scapulam
    Christian identity in Carthage in, 10–11, 14, 16
    on persecution of Christians, 35, 38–39, 40–42, 60
  Ad uxorem, 11–12, 16, 18, 32
  Apologeticum, 7

  abstention, Christians recognized by, 18–19
  on agape (weekly evening gathering), 15
  association, identification of Christians by, 14
  on cemeteries, 16–17
  conversion of individual Christians, gossip about, 17
  on occupations of Christians, 32
  on persecution of Christians, 36–38
  on treatment of sinners, 12
  association, Christians chiefly identified by, 14–17
  biographical information about Tertullian, 9–10
  charitable activities of Christians in, 16, 32–33
  Christianness as interpretive framework, Tertullian's imposition of, 92
  clothing, significance of, 13, 23–25
  De corona militis, 18, 40, 43–44
  De cultu feminarum, 9, 23–25
  De fuga in persecutione, 15, 44, 45–46
  De idololatria, 7, 9, 25–31
    Avodah Zarah and, 94
    betrothals and weddings, Christian attendance at, 28–29
    on education of Christians, 26, 31–32
    festivities public and private, Christian engagement in, 27–29
    imperial cult, Christian nonobservance of, 20, 28
    on impossibility of avoiding idolatry, 30
    military service, 29
    occupations involving idolatry, 25–27
    pollution, Christian attitudes toward, 22, 23
    speech, idolatry in, 29–30
    on what constitutes idolatry, 23, 25–31
  De pallio, 13
  De pudicitia, 12
  De spectaculis, 9, 14, 20–23, 24
  De virginibus velandis, 13
  defining Christian membership in, 11
  evidence for, 6
  external markers of Christianness in, lack of, 13–14
  festivities public and private, Christian engagement in, 27–29, 68–70
  idolatry, what constitutes, 23, 25–31
  imperial cult, Christian abstention from, 19–20, 28
  kiss as greeting amongst Christians, 17

Tertullian *(cont.)*
  liturgical events in, 15–16, 100n4–5
  loss of Christian membership in, 12
  ludi, Christian participation in/
    abstention from, 14, 19, 20–23,
    27–29
  maintaining Christian membership
    in, 11–12
  on marriage
    betrothals and weddings, Christians
      attendance at, 28–29
    between Christians and non-Christians,
      11–12, 16, 18, 32
  military service, Christian involvement
    in, 29, 43–44
  mutual social assistance between
    Christians in, 32–33
  nonreligious dictates of behavior,
    recognition of, 24–25
  occupations of Christians in, 13, 25–27, 32
  organization and number of Christians
    in Carthage, 10–11, 41–42, 100n2
  persecution of Christians in. *See under*
    persecution and Christian identity
  pollution, Christian beliefs about, 22–23
  problem, Christian life in pagan society
    viewed as, 9, 31
  Scorpiace, 44–45
  scripture, Christian use of, 22, 23–24
  separate "Christian world," existence of,
    31–33
  sign of the cross, as Christian gesture, 18
  speech, idolatry in, 29–30
  women's chastity and personal
    adornment, connection between,
    23–25
theatergoing, Augustine's condemnation of,
  66, 77–78
Theodosian age, Christian identity in. *See*
  Augustine and Christian identity
Theodosian Code, 62
trade, Christians engaging in, 26–27
Trajan (Roman emperor), 19
turificati, 103n31

Valentinians, 44, 45, 102n23
Valerian's persecution (257-260), 55–57
Van Winden, Jacobus, 25
Victor (lector and confessor), 52
Vigellius Saturninus (proconsul), 35
Virgil, 83
Volusianus (correspondent of Augustine),
  81–82

Waszink, Jan, 25
women's clothing and adornment,
  significance of, 13, 23–25

Yasin, Ann Marie, 104n5–6

Zenobius (friend of Augustine), 80,
  106n16

www.ingramcontent.com/pod-product-compliance
Lightning Source LLC
Chambersburg PA
CBHW020748230426
43665CB00009B/537